W

EPIDEMICS

OPPOSING VIEWPOINTS®

OTHER BOOKS OF RELATED INTEREST

EPIDEMICS

O P P O S I N G   V I E W P O I N T S®

William Dudley, Book Editor

David L. Bender, Publisher
Bruno Leone, Executive Editor
Bonnie Szumski, Editorial Director
Brenda Stalcup, Managing Editor
Scott Barbour, Senior Editor

OPPOSING
VIEWPOINTS®
SERIES

Greenhaven Press, Inc., San Diego, California

W

Library of Congress Cataloging-in-Publication Data

Epidemics : opposing viewpoints / William Dudley, book editor.
　　p.　　cm. — (Opposing viewpoints series)
　　Includes bibliographical references and index.
　　ISBN 1-56510-941-4 (lib. : alk. paper). —
ISBN 1-56510-940-6 (pbk. : alk. paper)
　　1. Epidemics—Social aspects. 2. AIDS (Disease)—Prevention.
3. Vaccination—Government policy. I. Dudley, William, 1964–
II. Series: Opposing viewpoints series (Unnumbered)
RA651.E661　1999
614.4—dc21
　　　　　　　　　　　　　　　　　　　　　　　　　98-28458
　　　　　　　　　　　　　　　　　　　　　　　　　CIP

Greenhaven Press, Inc., P.O. Box 289009
San Diego, CA 92198-9009

"CONGRESS SHALL MAKE NO LAW...ABRIDGING THE FREEDOM OF SPEECH, OR OF THE PRESS."

First Amendment to the U.S. Constitution

The basic foundation of our democracy is the First Amendment guarantee of freedom of expression. The Opposing Viewpoints Series is dedicated to the concept of this basic freedom and the idea that it is more important to practice it than to enshrine it.

CONTENTS

WHY CONSIDER OPPOSING VIEWPOINTS?

"The only way in which a human being can make some
approach to knowing the whole of a subject is by hearing
what can be said about it by persons of every variety of
opinion and studying all modes in which it can be looked
at by every character of mind. No wise man ever acquired
his wisdom in any mode but this."

John Stuart Mill

In our media-intensive culture it is not difficult to find differing
opinions. Thousands of newspapers and magazines and dozens
of radio and television talk shows resound with differing points
of view. The difficulty lies in deciding which opinion to agree
with and which "experts" seem the most credible. The more in-
undated we become with differing opinions and claims, the
more essential it is to hone critical reading and thinking skills to
evaluate these ideas. Opposing Viewpoints books address this
problem directly by presenting stimulating debates that can be
used to enhance and teach these skills. The varied opinions contained in each book examine many different aspects of a single
issue. While examining these conveniently edited opposing
views, readers can develop critical thinking skills such as the
ability to compare and contrast authors' credibility, facts, argu-
mentation styles, use of persuasive techniques, and other stylis-
tic tools. In short, the Opposing Viewpoints Series is an ideal
way to attain the higher-level thinking and reading skills so essential in a culture of diverse and contradictory opinions.

In addition to providing a tool for critical thinking, Opposing
Viewpoints books challenge readers to question their own
strongly held opinions and assumptions. Most people form their
opinions on the basis of upbringing, peer pressure, and personal, cultural, or professional bias. By reading carefully bal-
anced opposing views, readers must directly confront new ideas
as well as the opinions of those with whom they disagree. This
is not to simplistically argue that everyone who reads opposing
views will—or should—change his or her opinion. Instead, the
series enhances readers' understanding of their own views by
encouraging confrontation with opposing ideas. Careful examination of others' views can lead to the readers' understanding of
the logical inconsistencies in their own opinions, perspective on

why they hold an opinion, and the consideration of the possibility that their opinion requires further evaluation.

EVALUATING OTHER OPINIONS

To ensure that this type of examination occurs, Opposing Viewpoints books present all types of opinions. Prominent spokespeople on different sides of each issue as well as well-known professionals from many disciplines challenge the reader. An additional goal of the series is to provide a forum for other, less known, or even unpopular viewpoints. The opinion of an ordinary person who has had to make the decision to cut off life support from a terminally ill relative, for example, may be just as valuable and provide just as much insight as a medical ethicist's professional opinion. The editors have two additional purposes in including these less known views. One, the editors encourage readers to respect others' opinions—even when not enhanced by professional credibility. It is only by reading or listening to and objectively evaluating others' ideas that one can determine whether they are worthy of consideration. Two, the inclusion of such viewpoints encourages the important critical thinking skill of objectively evaluating an author's credentials and bias. This evaluation will illuminate an author's reasons for taking a particular stance on an issue and will aid in readers' evaluation of the author's ideas.

As series editors of the Opposing Viewpoints Series, it is our hope that these books will give readers a deeper understanding of the issues debated and an appreciation of the complexity of even seemingly simple issues when good and honest people disagree. This awareness is particularly important in a democratic society such as ours in which people enter into public debate to determine the common good. Those with whom one disagrees should not be regarded as enemies but rather as people whose views deserve careful examination and may shed light on one's own.

Thomas Jefferson once said that "difference of opinion leads to inquiry, and inquiry to truth." Jefferson, a broadly educated man, argued that "if a nation expects to be ignorant and free . . . it expects what never was and never will be." As individuals and as a nation, it is imperative that we consider the opinions of others and examine them with skill and discernment. The Opposing Viewpoints Series is intended to help readers achieve this goal.

David L. Bender & Bruno Leone,
Series Editors

Greenhaven Press anthologies primarily consist of previously published material taken from a variety of sources, including periodicals, books, scholarly journals, newspapers, government documents, and position papers from private and public organizations. These original sources are often edited for length and to ensure their accessibility for a young adult audience. The anthology editors also change the original titles of these works in order to clearly present the main thesis of each viewpoint and to explicitly indicate the opinion presented in the viewpoint. These alterations are made in consideration of both the reading and comprehension levels of a young adult audience. Every effort is made to ensure that Greenhaven Press accurately reflects the original intent of the authors included in this anthology.

INTRODUCTION

> "Remarkable achievements have been accomplished in the
> control of many epidemic infectious diseases in this century."
> —American Medical Association's Council on Scientific Affairs

> "AIDS does not stand alone; it may well be just the first of
> the modern, large-scale epidemics of infectious disease."
> —Laurie Garrett

Epidemics have been a major and recurring part of human history. Bubonic plague, caused by the bacterium *Yersinia pestis*, killed three quarters of Europe's population in the fourteenth century. Epidemics of such diseases as smallpox, yellow fever, and tuberculosis routinely swept through U.S. cities prior to the twentieth century. As recently as 1919, a fatal form of influenza spread through much of the world, killing as many as 20 million people worldwide, including a half-million Americans.

During the twentieth century, however, the advent of modern medicine—including the development of the disciplines of microbiology and immunology, the discovery and invention of vaccines and antibiotics, and the establishment of public health agencies—promised to make recurring epidemics a thing of the past. Vaccination campaigns helped to eradicate smallpox from the United States and eventually the entire world. Pneumonia and tuberculosis, two bacteria-caused infectious diseases that accounted for almost one quarter of all U.S. deaths in 1900, were the cause of less than 4 percent of U.S. deaths in 1990. In 1967 America's leading public health official, U.S. surgeon general William H. Stewart, proclaimed that "the war against infectious diseases has been won" and said that public health resources should instead be concentrated on chronic noninfectious diseases such as cancer and heart disease.

Stewart's pronouncement was premature. Disease epidemics have remained a significant—and growing—problem in the world. Infectious diseases killed more than 16.5 million people in 1993—a number greater than the combined death toll from cancer and heart disease combined—and accounted for 32 percent of global mortality. In addition, millions more people annually become sick with infectious diseases but do not die.

While epidemics remain a bigger problem in poor and undeveloped countries than in the United States, many observers argue that the potential threat they pose does not respect national boundaries in this era of global travel, migration, and commerce. Asian ships dropping ballast water started a cholera epidemic in Latin America. An outbreak of malaria, a parasitic disease spread by mosquitoes that is normally found only outside the United States, occurred in New Jersey in 1994; its source was believed to be immigrants from Asia or Latin America. Infectious diseases accounted for 166,000 deaths in 1992 in the United States, 8 percent of total U.S. fatalities. According to the Centers for Disease Control and Prevention (CDC), the U.S. death rate due to infectious diseases rose 58 percent between 1980 and 1992.

A major factor in the persistence—and resurgence—of infectious disease has been antibiotic resistance. Ever since penicillin was first made available for clinical use in 1944, it and other antibiotics have transformed many ominous diseases, including tuberculosis and syphilis, into mere inconveniences that could be cured with shots or pills. However, bacteria have proven to be extraordinarily adaptive and have evolved strains against which penicillin and other traditional antibiotics are ineffective. In addition to reproducing new generations every twenty minutes, many bacteria gain resistance by sharing genetic information with each other. Moreover, antibiotics actually help more resistant bacteria survive by killing off their competitors. "The more you use antibiotics," states George Curlin of the National Institute of Allergy and Infectious Diseases, "the more rapidly Mother Nature adapts to them." The result has been an explosion of drug-resistant strains of bacteria that cause pneumonia, tuberculosis, and other illnesses.

Many scientists worry that drug companies are failing to develop new antibiotics in time to keep up with the ability of bacteria to develop resistance, leaving humans exposed to possibly fatal infections, especially in hospitals. Barry R. Bloom, a professor of immunology and microbiology, noted in 1995 that after Staphylococcus bacteria became resistant to penicillin, they were treated with a replacement, methicillin. "Now there is a category of methicillin-resistant staph," he stated, "and we treat them with vancomycin. If this fails to work, we'll have to shut down the surgery wards." In the summer of 1997 many in the medical community were alarmed when two patients in the United States did become infected with a vancomycin-resistant, potentially fatal bacteria, *Staphylococcus aureus*. Deaths due to infections caught at U.S. hospitals rose from 19,000 in 1992 to 88,000 in 1997. Stuart B. Levy, director of the Center for Adaptation Genetics and Drug Resistance at Tufts University School of Medicine, argues that "we are on the road to an impending public health disaster" because of antibiotic resistance.

However, not all scientists and observers fully share this pessimistic view. Some point out that after a period of relative neglect, drug companies are again pouring resources into antibiotic research and development. Moreover, new techniques in genetic manipulation and analysis are helping them to develop a new generation of antibiotics. Physician and writer Anthony Daniels asserts that even a worst-case scenario of antibiotic failure will not necessarily result in a resurgence of epidemics—as long as sanitation measures are maintained. "A bacteriologically pure water supply," he writes, "is a better defense against waterborne diseases . . . than all the antibiotics in the world. The idea that, without antibiotics which work, we should necessarily return to primitive conditions is false."

Some critics argue that the dangers of diseases in general have been sensationalized in books, articles, and motion pictures such as Outbreak, a fictional account of a deadly epidemic in the United States. "The public perception from media reports is that the threat to general health caused by infectious diseases is as great today as at any time in the nation's history," writes the American Medical Association's Council on Scientific Affairs. "This conclusion is far from the truth." The council argues that the public should remain aware of the successes that vaccines and public health departments have had in reducing infectious disease incidents in the United States and worldwide. People should not panic or become resigned to epidemics, the council concludes, although they should maintain support for disease surveillance, vaccination research, and other public health efforts.

Whether epidemic diseases in this era of antibiotic resistance are a critical or exaggerated problem is one of several matters debated in Epidemics: Opposing Viewpoints, which contains the following chapters: Do Infectious Diseases Pose a Significant Threat to Humanity? What Can Be Done to Curtail the AIDS Epidemic? Are Government Vaccination Programs Beneficial? How Can Food-Borne Illnesses Be Prevented? The authors in this volume examine the resurgent problem of infectious disease in the United States and the world and discuss how governments and individuals should respond to the real and potential threats posed by epidemics.

CHAPTER 1

DO INFECTIOUS DISEASES POSE A SIGNIFICANT THREAT TO HUMANITY?

CHAPTER PREFACE

Michael Crichton's 1969 novel *The Andromeda Strain* tells of a space-based organism that is brought back to earth by a crashed satellite. The mysterious crystalline life form instantaneously kills almost every person it comes into contact with. *The Andromeda Strain* is a work of fiction, but many have wondered if a similar scenario could happen in real life—whether an undiscovered or newly mutated virus or other organism (not necessarily from space) could create a worldwide epidemic or even human extinction. Indeed, the term "Andromeda strain" itself has come into common usage to describe such an entity.

Some people consider the Ebola virus a potential real-life Andromeda strain. First discovered in Africa in 1976, its origins remain a mystery. The virus, for which there is no cure or vaccine, kills people gruesomely by clotting their blood and dissolving internal organs. Its potential for creating epidemics is limited by the fact that it is not spread through the air (as many viruses are), but through direct contact with blood or other bodily fluids. However, some fear the Ebola virus could mutate into a more easily transmissible form, as happened during a 1989 Ebola outbreak in a population of research monkeys in a facility in Reston, Virginia. Scientists there discovered to their horror that the virus apparently had mutated into a form that could be spread through airborne transmission. Several research workers became infected, but luckily this strain of Ebola proved fatal only to monkeys.

Other scientists and observers have questioned whether the Ebola virus is truly a candidate for Andromeda strain status. They point out that the virus is hard to catch and that it acts too quickly to create a widespread epidemic (victims become symptomatic and die before they can spread the disease to others). Skeptics argue that Ebola outbreaks among humans have occurred only in impoverished cities where elementary health and safety precautions were lacking, such as in Kikwit, Zaire (Congo), in 1995. "As deadly as it is," writes *Newsweek* reporter Geoffrey Cowley, "Ebola is ill equipped to go global, and humanity is well equipped to stop it."

Is humanity at risk of a worldwide viral epidemic? The viewpoints in this chapter examine the Ebola virus and other microorganisms and the potential threat they pose to humanity.

| "Medical experts now recognize that any microbe, including ones previously unknown to science, can . . . become a global threat."

INFECTIOUS DISEASES POSE A SIGNIFICANT THREAT TO HUMANITY

Laurie Garrett

Laurie Garrett is a science and health writer for *Newsday* and the author of the book *The Coming Plague: Newly Emerging Diseases in a World Out of Balance*. In the following viewpoint, Garrett argues that the belief held by many American and European health professionals in the 1960s and 1970s that infectious diseases would soon be conquered by antibiotics, vaccines, and other medical advances has proven to be unfounded. Microbes have developed resistance to antibiotics, she points out, while social developments in poor countries, including wars, refugee movements, and growing cities with little infrastructure, have provided new breeding grounds for disease. Furthermore, she contends, global migration and commercial air travel have made it impossible for outbreaks of disease to be confined to one place. The cumulative result of these developments has been a crisis of infectious diseases that threatens every country in the world, Garrett concludes.

As you read, consider the following questions:

1. Past optimism about infectious disease rested on which two false assumptions, according to Garrett?
2. What conditions make cities likely incubators and spreaders of disease, as described by the author?

S ince World War II, public health strategy has focused on the eradication of microbes. Using powerful medical weaponry developed during the postwar period—antibiotics, antimalarials, and vaccines—political and scientific leaders in the United States and around the world pursued a military-style campaign to obliterate viral, bacterial, and parasitic enemies. The goal was nothing less than pushing humanity through what was termed the "health transition," leaving the age of infectious disease permanently behind. By the turn of the century, it was thought, most of the world's population would live long lives ended only by the "chronics"—cancer, heart disease, and Alzheimer's.

The optimism culminated in 1978 when the member states of the United Nations signed the "Health for All, 2000" accord. The agreement set ambitious goals for the eradication of disease, predicting that even the poorest nations would undergo a health transition before the millennium, with life expectancies rising markedly. It was certainly reasonable in 1978 to take a rosy view of Homo sapiens' ancient struggle with the microbes; antibiotics, pesticides, chloroquine and other powerful antimicrobials, vaccines, and striking improvements in water treatment and food preparation technologies had provided what seemed an imposing armamentarium. The year before, the World Health Organization (WHO) had announced that the last known case of smallpox had been tracked down in Ethiopia and cured.

TWO FALSE ASSUMPTIONS

The grandiose optimism rested on two false assumptions: that microbes were biologically stationary targets and that diseases could be geographically sequestered. Each contributed to the smug sense of immunity from infectious diseases that characterized health professionals in North America and Europe.

Anything but stationary, microbes and the insects, rodents, and other animals that transmit them are in a constant state of biological flux and evolution. Charles Darwin noted that certain genetic mutations allow plants and animals to better adapt to environmental conditions and so produce more offspring; this process of natural selection, he argued, was the mechanism of evolution. Less than a decade after the U.S. military first supplied penicillin to its field physicians in the Pacific theater, geneticist Joshua Lederberg demonstrated that natural selection was operating in the bacterial world. Strains of staphylococcus and streptococcus that happened to carry genes for resistance to the drugs arose and flourished where drug-susceptible strains had been driven out. Use of antibiotics was selecting for ever-more-resistant bugs.

18

The emergence of AIDS, Ebola, and any number of other rain-forest agents appears to be a natural consequence of the ruin of the tropical biosphere. The emerging viruses are surfacing from ecologically damaged parts of the earth. Many of them come from the tattered edges of tropical rain forest, or they come from tropical savanna that is being settled rapidly by people. The tropical rain forests are the deep reservoirs of life on the planet, containing most of the world's plant and animal species. The rain forests are also its largest reservoirs of viruses, since all living things carry viruses. When viruses come out of an ecosystem, they tend to spread in waves through the human population, like echoes from the dying biosphere. . . .

In a sense, the earth is mounting an immune response against the human species. It is beginning to react to the human parasite, the flooding infection of people, the dead spots of concrete all over the planet, the cancerous rot-outs in Europe, Japan, and the United States, thick with replicating primates, the colonies enlarging and spreading and threatening to shock the biosphere with mass extinctions. Perhaps the biosphere does not "like" the idea of five billion humans. Or it could also be said that the extreme amplification of the human race, which has occurred only in the past hundred years or so, has suddenly produced a very large quantity of meat, which is sitting everywhere in the biosphere and may not be able to defend itself against a life form that might want to consume it. Nature has interesting ways of balancing itself. The rain forest has its own defenses. The earth's immune system, so to speak, has recognized the presence of the human species and is starting to kick in. The earth is attempting to rid itself of an infection by the human parasite. Perhaps AIDS is the first step in a natural process of clearance.

Richard Preston, *The Hot Zone*, 1994.

More recently scientists have witnessed an alarming mechanism of microbial adaptation and change—one less dependent on random inherited genetic advantage. The genetic blueprints of some microbes contain DNA and RNA codes that command mutation under stress, offer escapes from antibiotics and other drugs, marshal collective behaviors conducive to group survival, and allow the microbes and their progeny to scour their environments for potentially useful genetic material. Such material is present in stable rings or pieces of DNA and RNA, known as plasmids and transposons, that move freely among microorganisms, even jumping between species of bacteria, fungi, and parasites. Some plasmids carry the genes for resistance to five or more different families of antibiotics, or dozens of individual drugs. Others confer greater powers of infectivity, virulence, resistance to disinfectants or chlorine, even such subtly important characteristics as the ability to tolerate higher temperatures or more acidic conditions. Microbes have appeared that can grow on a bar of soap, swim unabashed in bleach, and ignore doses of penicillin logarithmically larger than those effective in 1950.

In the microbial soup, then, is a vast, constantly changing lending library of genetic material that offers humanity's minute predators myriad ways to outmaneuver the drug arsenal. And the arsenal, large as it might seem, is limited. In 1994 the Food and Drug Administration licensed only three new antimicrobial drugs, two of them for the treatment of AIDS and none an antibacterial. Research and development has ground to a near halt now that the easy approaches to killing viruses, bacteria, fungi, and parasites—those that mimic the ways competing microbes kill one another in their endless tiny battles throughout the human gastrointestinal tract—have been exploited. Researchers have run out of ideas for countering many microbial scourges, and the lack of profitability has stifled the development of drugs to combat organisms that are currently found predominantly in poor countries. "The pipeline is dry. We really have a global crisis," James Hughes, director of the National Center for Infectious Diseases at the Centers for Disease Control and Prevention (CDC) in Atlanta, said recently.

DISEASES WITHOUT BORDERS

During the 1960s, 1970s, and 1980s, the World Bank and the International Monetary Fund devised investment policies based on the assumption that economic modernization should come first and improved health would naturally follow. Today the World Bank recognizes that a nation in which more than ten percent of the working-age population is chronically ill cannot be expected to reach higher levels of development without investment in health infrastructure. Furthermore, the bank acknowledges that few societies spend health care dollars effectively for the poor, among whom the potential for the outbreak of infectious disease is greatest. Most of the achievements in infectious disease control have resulted from grand international efforts such as the expanded program for childhood immunization mounted by the U.N. Children's Emergency Fund and WHO's smallpox eradication drive. At the local level, particularly in politically unstable poor countries, few genuine successes can be cited.

Geographic sequestration was crucial in all postwar health planning, but diseases can no longer be expected to remain in their country or region of origin. Even before commercial air travel, swine flu in 1918–19 managed to circumnavigate the planet five times in 18 months, killing 22 million people, 500,000 in the United States. How many more victims could a similarly lethal strain of influenza claim in 1996, when some half a billion passengers will board airline flights?

Every day one million people cross an international border. One million a week travel between the industrial and developing worlds. And as people move, unwanted microbial hitchhikers tag along. In the nineteenth century most diseases and infections that travelers carried manifested themselves during the long sea voyages that were the primary means of covering great distances. Recognizing the symptoms, the authorities at ports of entry could quarantine contagious individuals or take other action. In the age of jet travel, however, a person incubating a disease such as Ebola can board a plane, travel 12,000 miles, pass unnoticed through customs and immigration, take a domestic carrier to a remote destination, and still not develop symptoms for several days, infecting many other people before his condition is noticeable. . . .

THE CITY AS VECTOR

Population expansion raises the statistical probability that pathogens will be transmitted, whether from person to person or vector—insect, rodent, or other—to person. Human density is rising rapidly worldwide. Seven countries now have overall population densities exceeding 2,000 people per square mile, and 43 have densities greater than 500 people per square mile. (The U.S. average, by contrast, is 74.)

High density need not doom a nation to epidemics and unusual outbreaks of disease if sewage and water systems, housing, and public health provisions are adequate. The Netherlands, for example, with 1,180 people per square mile, ranks among the top 20 countries for good health and life expectancy. But the areas in which density is increasing most are not those capable of providing such infrastructural support. They are, rather, the poorest on earth. Even countries with low overall density may have cities that have become focuses for extraordinary overpopulation, from the point of view of public health. Some of these urban agglomerations have only one toilet for every 750 or more people.

Most people on the move around the world come to burgeoning metropolises like India's Surat (where pneumonic plague struck in 1994) and Zaire's [now the Democratic Republic of the Congo] Kikwit (site of the 1995 Ebola epidemic) that offer few fundamental amenities. These new centers of urbanization typically lack sewage systems, paved roads, housing, safe drinking water, medical facilities, and schools adequate to serve even the most affluent residents. They are squalid sites of destitution where hundreds of thousands live much as they would in poor villages, yet so jammed together as to ensure astronomical transmission rates for airborne, waterborne, sexually transmitted, and contact-transmission microbes.

A Competition with Microbes

Ultimately, humanity will have to change its perspective on its place in Earth's ecology if the species hopes to stave off or survive the next plague. . . .

As the Homo sapiens population swells, surging past the 6 billion mark at the millennium, the opportunities for pathogenic microbes multiply. If, as some have predicted, 100 million of those people might then be infected with HIV, the microbes will have an enormous pool of walking immune-deficient petri dishes in which to thrive, swap genes, and undergo endless evolutionary experiments.

"We are in an eternal competition. We have beaten out virtually every other species to the point where we may now talk about protecting our former predators," Joshua Lederberg told a 1994 Manhattan gathering of investment bankers. "But we're not alone at the top of the food chain."

Our microbe predators are adapting, changing, evolving, he warned. "And any more rapid change would be at the cost of human devastation.". . .

While the human race battles itself, fighting over ever more crowded turf and scarcer resources, the advantage moves to the microbes' court. They are our predators and they will be victorious if we, Homo sapiens, do not learn how to live in a rational global village that affords the microbes few opportunities.

It's either that or we brace ourselves for the coming plague.

Laurie Garrett, The Coming Plague: Newly Emerging Diseases in a World Out of Balance, 1994.

But such centers are often only staging areas for the waves of impoverished people that are drawn there. The next stop is a megacity with a population of ten million or more. In the nineteenth century only two cities on earth—London and New York—even approached that size. Five years from now there will be 24 megacities, most in poor developing countries: São Paulo, Calcutta, Bombay, Istanbul, Bangkok, Tehran, Jakarta, Cairo, Mexico City, Karachi, and the like. There the woes of cities like Surat are magnified many times over. Yet even the developing world's megacities are way stations for those who most aggressively seek a better life. All paths ultimately lead these people—and the microbes they may carry—to the United States, Canada, and Western Europe.

Urbanization and global migration propel radical changes in human behavior as well as in the ecological relationship between microbes and humans. Almost invariably in large cities, sex industries arise and multiple-partner sex becomes more common, prompting rapid increases in sexually transmitted diseases. Black market access to antimicrobials is greater in urban centers, leading to overuse or outright misuse of the precious drugs and the emergence of resistant bacteria and parasites. Intravenous drug abusers' practice of sharing syringes is a ready vehicle for the transmission of microbes. Underfunded urban health facilities often become unhygienic centers for the dissemination of disease rather than its control.

AIDS AND OTHER DISEASES

All these factors played out dramatically during the 1980s, allowing an obscure organism to amplify and spread to the point that WHO estimates it has infected a cumulative total of 30 million people and become endemic to every country in the world. Genetic studies of the human immunodeficiency virus that causes AIDS indicate that it is probably more than a century old, yet HIV infected perhaps less than .001 percent of the world population until the mid-1970s. Then the virus surged because of sweeping social changes: African urbanization; American and European intravenous drug use and homosexual bathhouse activity; the Uganda-Tanzania war of 1977–79, in which rape was used as a tool of ethnic cleansing; and the growth of the American blood products industry and the international marketing of its contaminated goods. Government denial and societal prejudice everywhere in the world led to inappropriate public health interventions or plain inaction, further abetting HIV transmission and slowing research for treatment or a cure.

The estimated direct (medical) and indirect (loss of productive labor force and family-impact) costs of the disease are expected to top $500 billion by the year 2000, according to the Global AIDS Policy Coalition at Harvard University. The U.S. Agency for International Development predicts that by then some 11 percent of children under 15 in sub-Saharan Africa will be AIDS orphans, and that infant mortality will soar fivefold in some African and Asian nations, due to the loss of parental care among children orphaned by AIDS and its most common opportunistic infection, tuberculosis. Life expectancy in the African and Asian nations hit hardest by AIDS will plummet to an astonishing low of 25 years by 2010, the agency forecasts.

Medical experts now recognize that any microbe, including ones previously unknown to science, can take similar advantage of conditions in human society, going from isolated cases camouflaged by generally high levels of disease to become a global threat. Furthermore, old organisms, aided by mankind's misuse of disinfectants and drugs, can take on new, more lethal forms.

A White House–appointed interagency working group on emerging and reemerging infectious diseases estimates that at least 29 previously unknown diseases have appeared since 1973 and 20 well-known ones have reemerged, often in new drug-resistant or deadlier forms. According to the group, total direct and indirect costs of infectious disease in the United States in 1993 were more than $120 billion; combined federal, state, and municipal government expenditures that year for infectious disease control were only $74.2 million (neither figure includes AIDS, other sexually transmitted diseases, or tuberculosis).

> "What we have learned about
> infectious disease suggests that we
> should not fear extinction."

THE THREAT OF INFECTIOUS DISEASES HAS BEEN OVERSTATED

Malcolm Gladwell

Two books published in 1994 prompted much discussion over emerging diseases: *The Hot Zone* by Richard Preston and *The Coming Plague* by Laurie Garrett. In the following viewpoint, Malcolm Gladwell, a staff writer for the *New Yorker* magazine and a former New York bureau chief for the *Washington Post* newspaper, examines the theory popularized by these books that emerging infectious diseases pose a significant threat to humanity. He criticizes the two works and similar writings for exaggerating the dangers of infectious diseases to humans and underestimating the abilities of the scientific and medical establishments to overcome them. Gladwell argues that the chances that a lethal and communicable "super-virus" could threaten humanity's existence are extremely remote.

As you read, consider the following questions:

1. In what ways is humanity better off with respect to infectious diseases than it was a century ago, according to Gladwell?
2. What is the relationship between humanity's disruptions of the environment and the outbreaks of disease, according to the author?
3. What are two of the specific criticisms the author makes of *The Hot Zone* and *The Coming Plague*?

In the spring of 1983, a flock of wild ducks carrying a strain of avian influenza virus settled on a pond in a chicken farm in eastern Pennsylvania. The virus was excreted in the ducks' feces, which meant that it got onto the ground and then onto the boots of a farmer, which is why in turn it soon found its way into the chicken barn. From there the virus spread, carried by truckers who go from farm to farm collecting eggs, selling feed or taking broilers to market. As it spread, it replicated hundreds of millions of times, and as it replicated it underwent a critical mutation that turned it from a relatively benign virus into a killer. By late spring, chickens were collapsing within days of infection. By October, 17 million domestic birds—broilers, layers, turkeys, guinea fowl—from Pennsylvania down though Maryland and Virginia were dead.

VIRUS PARANOIA

The great Pennsylvania chicken epidemic went largely unnoticed at the time. In 1983, people did not draw analogies between the health of domestic fowl and the health of the general public. But today is a different matter. The United States is in the grip of paranoia about viruses and diseases and what happened in Pennsylvania has acquired a certain symbolism. There has been a Hollywood film, a made-for-TV-movie, a cover story in Newsweek and countless news specials and media reports on the subject of killer viruses. In the spring of 1995, a small outbreak of the African Ebola virus in Zaire [now the Democratic Republic of the Congo] drew virtually every major news organization to the hitherto unknown city of Kikwit. Richard Preston's The Hot Zone, a terrifying tale of how close America came to a major epidemic of the Ebola virus in 1989, has been on The New York Times best-seller list for thirty-seven weeks [as of July 1995]. And a well-received tome about infectious disease has also arrived from Laurie Garrett, a science reporter for Newsday, which is filled with gloomy quotations like this one, from the Nobel Prize–winning biologist Joshua Lederberg: "Are we better off than we were a century ago? In most respects we are worse off. We have been neglectful of the microbes and that is a recurring theme that is coming back to haunt us."

In all of these books, movies and news reports there is a sense of fear: Americans have been well and properly frightened of viruses, after all, since the AIDS epidemic began in the early 1980s. But there is also a sense of helplessness, a feeling of fatedness, as if we are all somehow in the same position today as the chickens of the Northeast were in 1983. "The chicken population in Pennsylvania [in 1983] is like the world as it is in this moment," Robert G. Webster, one of the country's leading virologists, recently observed. "What would we have done if this virus had occurred in humans? There are millions of us 'chickens' just waiting to be infected."

What are the sources of this pessimism? . . .

Some of the blame clearly belongs with AIDS, the epidemic that has more or less shattered the public's confidence in the power of science. But AIDS has never been seen as a threat to the entire species. In fact, AIDS is exactly the opposite of the kind of random, uncontrollable epidemic that seems to have now seized the popular imagination. The truth is that it is very hard to find an adequate explanation for the current American obsession. Joshua Lederberg's comment that we are worse off today than a century ago is proof only that he is a better student of microbiology than of history.

How can we be worse off than we were at a time when the average American lived only into his 40s, and the hospitals were filled with concurrent epidemics of tuberculosis, acute rheumatic fever, smallpox, diphtheria, tetanus, polio and pneumonia? Ebola may be new and scary, but in the twenty years since its discovery it has killed no more than several hundred people. In fact, it is safe to say that more Zairians in Kikwit died of diarrhea in the spring of 1995 than of Ebola. Even the analogy to the Pennsylvania chickens, though it fits the current hysteria like a glove, is absurd. Human beings do not live their lives crammed next to each other in metal cages. They do not wallow in their own feces. They have the brains and the ability to take precautions against disease and contagion. People are not chickens. So why all of a sudden are we convinced that we are?

The Ebola Virus

African Ebola is one of the deadliest of known human viruses. It kills by clotting the blood of its victims, shutting off the flow of nutrients to key parts of the body and chewing through connective tissue, so that the infected literally cough their guts out. No one knows what animal serves as Ebola's natural host, but it can jump from species to species, from guinea pigs to humans, killing virtually everything it touches. There is no cure for Ebola. And there is no vaccine. On the three occasions that it has broken out among humans—twice in Zaire and once in the Sudan—it has left behind a trail of death. Only once [as of 1995] has Ebola made its way to North America and that occasion is the basis of Richard Preston's *The Hot Zone*. . . .

What makes the book so interesting, and helps to account for its extraordinary popularity, is the manner in which Preston manages to turn the story of Ebola into an ecological parable. This is not only a medical warning, it is also an environmental warning. In Preston's hands, epidemiology leads directly to a kind of Luddism. For the new killer viruses of the African rainforest, he believes, represent nature's response to humanity's environmental crimes.

ENVIRONMENTAL IRRESPONSIBILITY?

This is an argument that rose to prominence with the emergence of AIDS. HIV, the theory goes, probably lived for millennia in the jungles of Africa, peacefully co-existing with its natural animal host. From time to time, it may have jumped into humans, making a brief run, say, through a jungle village, but it stayed in the rainforest. Then came the massive environmental upheaval of the 1970s. Truck routes were built into the continental interior. The Ugandan-Tanzanian war, which took place at the center of where monkey-borne HIV is thought to reside, uprooted entire populations. Cities began to spill over into what had been virgin territory, bringing with them new patterns of sexual behavior and prostitution. The effect was to give HIV a clear route out of the jungle. And what happened with AIDS, Preston says, is what is now happening with Ebola, and may soon happen again with something infinitely nastier than either of them.

Laurie Garrett takes this argument one step further. In The Coming Plague, her 750-page opus, she is not concerned just with rainforest viruses. She maintains that toxic shock syndrome, Legionnaires' disease, the rise of antibiotic-resistant infections, Lassa fever, Hantaan virus and virtually every other microbial outbreak of the past twenty years are all linked by the same pattern of environmental irresponsibility. "Ultimately humanity will have to change its perspective on its place in Earth's ecology if the species hopes to stave off or survive the next plague," she concludes. In the world of microbes,

> human beings stomp about with swagger, elbowing their way without concern into one ecosphere after another. The human race seems equally complacent about blazing a path into a rainforest with bulldozers and arson or using an antibiotic "scorched earth" policy to chase unwanted microbes across the duodenum.

This idea clearly has its roots in the environmentalism of the 1980s. Then we were told that destroying the rainforest would irreparably alter our climate. Now we are told that it will destroy our health. This revision, however, is not trivial. If the environmentalist warnings failed to ignite mass fear or mass politics, it was because they were so abstract. For how long could a series of speculative scientific projections about long-term trends toward warmer weather (of all the terrifying fates!) hold the public's attention? But the new virus paranoia puts the old global warming paranoia to shame. This is not a prediction. It is a judgment. We have wronged nature and it will exact its revenge. . . .

A LONGSTANDING STRUGGLE

What should we make of all this? Is nature really about to teach humanity a lesson? The answer depends in large part on whether you are an optimist or a pessimist, and on the magnitude of your faith in the power of medical science to respond quickly to new problems. But it should be said, first of all, that nature has been striking back against the ceaseless explorations and expansions of human beings, against [what Preston calls] the "human parasite," for as long as men have roamed the earth.

In *Plagues and Peoples*, which appeared in 1977, William McNeill pointed out that . . . while man's efforts to "remodel" his environment are sometimes a source of new disease, they are seldom a source of serious epidemic disease. Quite the opposite. As humans and new microorganisms interact, they begin to accommodate each other. Human populations slowly build up resistance to circulating infections. What were once virulent infections, such as syphilis, become attenuated. Over time, diseases of adults, such as measles and chicken pox, become limited to children, whose immune systems are still naïve. . . .

THE INFECTION PARADOX

This, says McNeill, is the paradox of infection: "The more diseased a community, the less destructive its epidemics become." Who, after all, suffered the most from the discovery of the New World? Not the conquerors, the ones who were despoiling a virgin environment. It was the conquered, the American Indians, the peoples living on a secluded and pristine continent, who were all but wiped out by the sudden arrival of smallpox. This does not mean, of course, that we should not worry about the effects of man's continuing assault on nature. But it does mean that there is nothing inherently terrifying about the fact that the West is now being exposed to new microbes from equatorial Africa. We are ultimately safer in a world where new viruses and bacteria are in constant circulation, and where human populations can encounter and build defenses against them. Unlocking the viruses of the rainforest is part of the way we tame nature, not the way nature tames us.

One can go further. Sometimes disrupting the environment is the way we get rid of disease. In England in the seventeenth century, for example, farmers began disrupting nature by raising livestock on a large scale for the first time. What happened? Malaria-carrying mosquitoes, which used to feed on people, switched to cattle. And since cattle aren't an hospitable host for the malarial plasmodium, the disease, which had been endemic in Britain for centuries, retreated from the British Isles for good. . . .

HUMANITY FIGHTS BACK

Experts say humanity is now at a crucial turning point in the millennia-old war against microbes. One reason is the explosion in world population. Another is air travel—the deadliest infectious diseases are only a plane ride away from New York, London, or Tokyo.

Most ominously, though, microbes have been hard at work in a deadly race, mutating to create potent new defenses far beyond the reach of many existing treatments. . . .

But microbes aren't the planet's only wily species—and humanity is fighting back. One part of the solution is to beef up global surveillance and respond faster to diseases, squelching outbreaks before they explode into epidemics. A second is boosting prevention. . . .

The final piece of the puzzle is the development of new drugs and vaccines. . . . Top researchers at Wyeth-Ayerst, Pfizer, Abbott Laboratories, Merck, SmithKline Beecham, Glaxo Wellcome, Schering-Plough, and a host of biotech companies are launching an assault against infectious disease. . . .

Fueling the hope for better treatments are rapid advances in technology that speed up drug discovery. Robotics and high-speed equipment allow researchers to test thousands of compounds against a disease target in one day. And the gene-sleuthing revolution has made it possible to finally understand what makes bugs tick—and how to attack them at their most vulnerable points. "We are stripping these beasts bare, exposing their genetic secrets, and turning that information against them," says Alan R. Proctor, an executive director of research at Pfizer Inc.

Amy Barrett et al., *Business Week*, April 6, 1998.

The point is that the relationship between environment and disease is a complicated one. There are diseases that are caused by environmental disruption, diseases that are eliminated by environmental disruption and diseases whose rise has nothing to do with environmental disruption. The current plague paranoia is an obsession with the first category. Thus Garrett is very convincing when she talks about how the new cities of the Third World—overpopulated, vastly underserved by medical care, troubled by appalling sanitary conditions—are breeding grounds for new infections. But this is not an accurate diagnosis of all new diseases. . . .

Should We Be Scared?

But these are, to some extent, side issues. There is no question that for whatever reason, as a result of what man does to himself or what he does to his environment, the threat of infectious disease is on the rise in the world right now. The re-emergence of tuberculosis and untreatable strains of malaria, for example, are worrisome trends. Should we be scared? Well, yes and no. In his brilliant study, *Evolution of Infectious Disease*, Paul Ewald describes how the chaos at the end of the First World War directly contributed to the rise of an unusually vicious strain of influenza. The result was the influenza pandemic of 1918, which left 20 million people dead. This could happen again. But whether or not some new virus could emerge that could wipe us all out is an entirely different matter. It is simply very difficult to imagine where such a super-virus would come from or what it would look like. . . .

Every infectious agent that has ever plagued humanity has had to adopt a specific strategy, but every strategy carries a corresponding cost, and this makes human counterattack possible. Malaria is vicious and deadly, but it relies on mosquitoes to spread from one human to the next, which means that draining swamps and putting up mosquito netting can all but halt endemic malaria. Smallpox is extraordinarily durable, remaining infectious in the environment for years, but its very durability, its essential rigidity, is what makes it one of the easiest microbes to create a vaccine against. AIDS is almost invariably lethal because it attacks the body at its point of great vulnerability, that is, the immune system, but the fact that it targets blood cells is what makes it so relatively uninfectious.

Viruses Are Not Superhuman

I could go on, but the point is obvious. Any microbe capable of wiping us all out would have to be everything at once: as contagious as flu, as durable as the cold, as lethal as Ebola, as stealthy as HIV and so doggedly resistant to mutation that it would stay deadly over the course of a long epidemic. But viruses are not, well, superhuman. They cannot do everything at once. It is one of the ironies of the analysis of alarmists such as Preston that they are all too willing to point out the limitations of human beings, but they neglect to point out the limitations of microscopic life forms.

If there are any conclusions to be drawn about disease, they are actually the opposite of what is imagined in books such as *The Hot Zone* and *The Coming Plague*. It is true that the effect of the dramatic demographic and social changes in the world over the past few decades is to create new opportunities for disease. But they are likely to create not homogeneous patterns of disease, as humans experienced in the past, so much as heterogeneous patterns of disease. People are traveling more and living in different combinations. Gene pools that were once distinct are mixing through intermarriage. Adults who once would have died in middle age are now living into their 80s. Children with particular genetic configurations who once died at birth or in infancy are now living longer lives. If you talk to demographers, they will tell you that what they anticipate is increasing clusters of new and odd diseases moving into these new genetic and demographic niches. Rare diseases will be showing up in greater numbers. Entirely unknown diseases will emerge for the first time. But the same diversity that created them within those population subgroups will keep them there. Laurie Garrett's book is mistitled. We are not facing "the coming plague." We are facing "the coming outbreaks.". . .

The Coming Plague is almost entirely given over to description. For 600 pages, Garrett brings science in all its glory to bear on the question of why the variety of scourges facing mankind arose just when they did. But when it comes to writing about solutions, she delivers twenty-five pages. And her final advice is so broad as to be useless: man must be nicer to nature. Books more scrupulous than Preston's and Garrett's would have pointed out that what we have learned about infectious disease suggests that we should not fear extinction, that our ability to understand a threat and act accordingly is what separates us from the chickens of Pennsylvania. But what we have been given, instead, and what we have accepted uncritically, is medicine in retreat, and science as the passive observer of events. In this incarnation, science excels only at making the unimaginable imaginable and the incomprehensible comprehensible. It does not inspire courage. It inspires fear. It is good at creating helplessness. It is not good at dispelling it.

> "The advance of society, the very
> science of change, has greatly
> augmented the potential for the
> emergence of a pandemic strain."

EMERGING VIRUSES MAY THREATEN HUMANITY WITH EXTINCTION

Frank Ryan

Frank Ryan, a British physician and writer, is the author of *The Forgotten Plague*, a study of tuberculosis, and *Virus X*, from which the following viewpoint is excerpted. Ryan examines why certain viruses, such as the Ebola virus, sometimes cause lethal outbreaks among humans and whether viruses could potentially cause the extinction of the human species. He theorizes that viruses have evolved to exist in a symbiotic relationship with many animals, causing no harm to their host but causing fatal illnesses to related animals that are potential competitors of the viral host. Therefore, he contends, primates and other animals may harbor viruses fatal to humans. The continuing expansion of humans into rain forests and other wilderness areas increases the chances of viral outbreaks, he asserts, while overcrowding in cities and other social developments might cause these outbreaks to become a worldwide epidemic. Ryan describes what characteristics a virus would have to possess in order to cause human extinction.

As you read, consider the following questions:

1. What is an "aggressive symbiont," according to Ryan?
2. What qualities of the AIDS virus cause the author great concern?

In the forests of Borneo grow species of rattan cane that have a symbiotic relationship with ants. The ants construct a nest around the cane and protect it from browsing herbivores. If the leaves are tugged, the ants swarm from their nests, first beating out a tattoo, rather like the warning of a rattlesnake. If the attack upon the cane continues, the ants charge out and sting the offending animal about its sensitive mouth parts. . . . In the savannahs that encircle the African rain forests, there are many varieties of acacia trees that rely on a similar symbiotic protection from ants. A browsing herbivore, such as a giraffe, is subjected to a remorseless stinging assault upon its tongue and lips until it ceases to damage the acacia. In return, the tree repays its protector with living quarters and a ready and consistent supply of sugary nectar. . . .

AGGRESSIVE SYMBIOSIS

This is a very common form of symbiosis. The contribution by the minuscule partner is not one of mutual provision of sustenance but aggression. For this reason I have termed it "aggressive symbiosis," though the aggression is not directed at the symbiotic partner but outward—"exogenously"—at a potential rival of the symbiotic partner. No biologist would question this as a classical example of symbiosis. So what is the difference to the situation where a virus protects its host in a similarly aggressive way? The host benefits from the reduced competition from a rival species, while the virus enjoys protection and the facility of replication within the host. The virus, like the ant in the acacia tree, is the "aggressive symbiont."

A striking example of such aggressive symbiosis is the behavior of herpes-B viruses in their infective relationships with primates. One such virus, *Herpesvirus saimiri*, has a coevolutionary relationship with the squirrel monkey, *Saimiri sciureus*, that lives in the Amazonian rain forest. If a rival species, for example, the marmoset monkey, which shares the same rain forest habitat, comes into contact with the squirrel monkey, the virus hops species to wipe out the entire rival species. Not only does the virus induce cancer, it does so with a voracious rapidity, the marmosets dying from a fulminating cancer of the lymphatic system.

A similar virus, *Herpesvirus ateles*, which coevolves with spider monkeys in the South American jungle, is also virtually 100 percent lethal to exposed monkeys from related but immunologically naive species.

The herpesvirus coevolving with the squirrel or spider monkeys is behaving exactly as one would expect of an exogenously aggressive symbiont in eliminating competition with its host for food and shelter in the local ecology. Maintained in the host species by vertical transmission through oral contact with virus-containing saliva, the virus is shed copiously over the monkey's ecology throughout its life. . . . Puzzled by the fact that the virus would not harm its host, scientists tried to force the virus to induce disease. Yet even when the natural host was immunologically suppressed with drugs, the virus could not be induced to harm it. Could anything have more dramatically illustrated the true symbiotic nature of the relationship! . . .

How Outbreaks Become Epidemics

If the hypothesis of aggressive symbiosis is correct, then the "accident" theory of viral attack on people, for example in the African Ebola outbreaks, is misleading. The attacking virus is programmed to injure and kill, even if in doing so this portion of the swarm sacrifices itself in an evolutionary cul-de-sac. The symbiotic relationship is well served by this sacrifice. This is as important as it is a radically different perception.

The Ebola and hantavirus outbreaks fit the first step in this integrated scenario. They are precisely what one would expect from aggressive symbiosis on the parts of the viruses. And if they have made humanity more wary of encroaching on the African rain forest, as such attacks may well have succeeded in doing in our hunter-gatherer past, they could be seen as biological successes. But Homo sapiens is no longer primarily a hunter-gatherer. We have radically moved the goalposts, with huge urban populations and a mobility that would have been impossible for animals in nature. And it is this that makes it possible, more rarely of course, but of immense human significance, for a combination of successful viral strategies, extreme infectiousness, and human behavior to produce the right circumstances for an epidemic in the new human host while the virus is still behaving as an aggressive symbiont.

What then are the circumstances that make it possible for such aggression to become epidemic?

Occasionally, the attacking virus discovers an avenue of contagion that enormously extends its penetration and infectiousness. This can arise from spread through a universal medium, such as food or water, through carriage by a common biting insect, or most dangerous of all, through spread in a highly efficient way from one member of the victim species to another. In human terms, the most extreme manifestation of such circumstances will take place when the aggressive symbiont, now termed an emerging virus, discovers the means of mounting a global attack. This is the most threatening scenario of all, an epidemic that sweeps across continents, referred to as a "pandemic."

Such an event took place in the late 1970s to produce the worst human catastrophe of the twentieth century when two immunodeficiency viruses, HIV-1 and HIV-2, long established as aggressive symbionts with their evolutionary partners, primates in the African rain forest, attacked an intruding rival species of primate—humanity—and discovered the venereal route as an efficient means of spread from person to person. The result was the AIDS pandemic. . . .

QUESTIONS WE MUST FACE

It is scary to view pandemics as a natural evolutionary program. Could such a pandemic virus, or a pandemic resulting from a change in an existing virus, threaten the whole human species? Such questions are almost too appalling to contemplate. Yet they must be faced. . . .

We know now that the most dangerous new pandemic is likely to be viral in origin; and the most likely trigger for the emergence of this virus will be human intrusion into a wilderness ecology. I no longer view the aggressive attack as random but designed . . . under the influence of evolutionary laws, to maximally injure and kill the transgressor. In previous history, this aggression would have eradicated the hunter band or primate troop, perhaps even the village they carried it back to, or the equivalent animal colony. We have witnessed what such pandemics do in nature, as in the examples of yellow fever in South American monkeys, or myxomatosis in Australian rabbits. . . .

Pandemics are inevitable. Our incredibly rapid human evolution, our overwhelming global needs, the advances of our complex industrial society, all have moved the natural goalposts. The advance of society, the very science of change, has greatly augmented the potential for the emergence of a pandemic strain. It is hardly surprising that Avrion Mitchison, scientific director of Deutsches Rheuma Forschungszentrum in Berlin, asks the question: "Will we survive?"

We have invaded every biome on earth and we continue to destroy other species so very rapidly that one eminent scientist foresees the day when no life exists on earth apart from the human monoculture and the small volume of species useful to it. An increasing multitude of disturbed viral-host symbiotic cycles are provoked into self-protective counterattacks. This is a dangerous situation. . . .

It begs the most frightening question of all: could such a pandemic virus cause the extinction of the human species? . . .

VIRUS X

In virological circles such a doomsday virus is often referred to as "the Andromeda strain," after the bestselling thriller by Michael Crichton. But this is a misnomer. The Andromeda strain was not a virus at all, but a crystalline entity that came to earth on a meteorite from outer space. . . . If ever an extinction strain does threaten the human species, it is more likely to be a virus, and it will emerge from the diversity of life on earth. For this reason, I have called it Virus X, with X the logical derivative of extinction. What would be the likely properties of such a virus?

To cause our extinction, Virus X would need to take two steps. First it would have to kill everybody, or almost everybody, it infected. The qualifier is needed because the end of human civilization might not require the death of all of its members. Has any virus, or any other infectious agent, ever caused such a lethality? The answer, unfortunately, is yes—though the emergence of such catastrophic lethality is rare. Rabies was uniformly lethal in humans for at least four thousand years of history until Louis Pasteur discovered the first vaccine treatment. . . .

HIV-1 still appears almost uniformly lethal, though occasional reports of survivors are now appearing, and the Zairian Ebola virus was a close rival, with 90 percent fatality to the people it infected. However, with HIV-1 and Ebola, the worry of a species threat is far greater than with rabies.

Could such lethal agents ever take the second step, and become sufficiently contagious to infect all or virtually all of the human species? The reassuring fact is that the vast majority of emerging viruses, including those with such huge lethality, fail in practice to become pandemic. We know some of the explanations. An infection directly contracted from an animal or biting insect will never pose such a problem because the numbers infected will be limited by the extent of contact. . . . Food- or water-borne epidemics, though they might infect large numbers of people, can be interrupted by appropriate recognition and introduced measures of hygiene. Even sexually transmitted disease, such as AIDS, can be controlled by mechanical prophylaxis and a reduction in promiscuity; and blood-borne infections by control of contaminated supply, syringes, and needles. As far as we are aware—and one always has to qualify extrapolation based on past experience with caution—the only route of contagion likely to prove universally threatening to humanity would be person-to-person spread by the respiratory route.

The potential for respiratory spread of a plague microbe is unique. Each adult inhales about 10,000 liters of air each day, and we cannot avoid inhaling one another's expired discharges. Given a few minutes in a crowded room, the infected individual will, by coughing or sneezing, transmit the microbe to many of the others present. This was seen most tragically and historically in the switch from bubonic to pneumonic plague during the Black Death. Notable among present-day viruses that spread with very high levels of contagion by the aerosol route are the rhinoviruses and corona viruses that cause common colds. We are all familiar with the rapid spread of the influenza virus, which has long proved its capability to cause pandemics. But to threaten our species, or to provoke a near enough catastrophe to destroy human civilization, a virus would need to combine the infectivity of influenza with the lethality of HIV-1 or Ebola Zaire. . . .

There are worrying indications of recent near misses. Lassa virus can localize in the throat but not in enough quantity to result in aerosol spread. A good deal more alarming is that same potential for Ebola. The studies being carried out at the United States Army Medical Research Institute of Infectious Diseases (USAMRIID) on the Ebola Reston are starkly illuminating.

THE EBOLA THREAT

There was abundant epidemiological evidence within the Hazelton monkey facility [near Reston, Virginia, where an Ebola outbreak occurred in 1989] for spread of the Ebola virus from room to room by aerosol. The pattern of illness in the monkeys was primarily a respiratory one, with running noses, coughing and sneezing, and a pneumonia at autopsy. . . .

The Ebola virus is widely regarded as the most dangerous acute virus to emerge in modern history. Though thankfully the Reston strain did not ignite a human epidemic, there was evidence it did cross the species barrier. No demonstration could more convincingly evoke the capacity of a newly emerged BSL-4 agent to combine its terrible lethality with respiratory spread.

THE AIDS THREAT

With AIDS too there is grounds for worry. Because the virus will not infect ordinary laboratory animals, a strain of immunologically deficient mice has been bred to permit study of the dynamics of infection. These mice, genetically altered to allow grafting with human lymphocytes [white blood cells], allow scientists to study the effects of HIV-1 in human cells grafted into the animals. In 1990 the research workers were shocked to discover that when the two HIV-1 viruses came together inside the infected cells they swapped parts of their genomes, creating new hybrids. In still more alarming instances, where the mice were coincidentally infected with their own retroviruses, the introduced HIV-1 viruses swapped part of their genomes, including the coding for structures such as the envelope proteins [virus surface proteins that help bind viruses to host cells], with the mouse "endogenous" retrovirus. This opened up a potential for radically altered hybrids. It also alarmed many eminent retrovirologists, including Howard Temin, who questioned the further use of mice in the investigation of AIDS in this way. Subsequent researches have confirmed that AIDS viruses are spectacularly "recombinogenic." Such juggling of genes between different AIDS viruses infecting the same patients is one of the reasons why an AIDS vaccine is proving so elusive.

Reprinted by permission of Bob Englehart.

Recombination between viruses is now regarded as one of the major pathways of viral evolution. It has worried a good many other scientists, including Professor Paul Sharp of Nottingham University: "I would not want to create a scare, but this ability to create hybrids gives you an evolutionary jump and we don't know what the properties of a hybrid may be." An escalation of concern arose from the finding by P. Lusso, Robert C. Gallo, and colleagues that HIV-1 viruses that had recombined with mouse leukemia virus inside transplanted human cells now had the capacity to infect cells from respiratory epithelium [cellular tissue]. While this new "tissue tropism" is still just a finding in the laboratory—and therefore a long way from reproducing an event in nature—it worries a great many experts, including Joshua Lederberg, Gallo, and Ed Kilbourne. It shows all too clearly that the worst-case scenario is possible: and that nobody can really predict the degree of certainty or uncertainty of its possibility. Even so, some scientists regard such thinking as apostasy, consoling themselves that if HIV were capable of infecting the respiratory epithelium it would not withstand drying and so would not be infectious to others through coughing or sneezing. But a new surface envelope, as a result of such recombination, might well alter the viral resistance to drying. And a modified virus would not need to survive long in air, particularly if kept moist for a short time in the aerosolized droplet, for transmission to prove successful in a crowded ambience.

Had HIV-1 spread by aerosol from the beginning, we would not even have registered its existence for several years, since symptoms of first infection are mild or nonexistent. This sinister spread would have precluded any effective public health measures. In such a dreadful circumstance, the global village, with its closely woven nexus of great cities, packed with utterly naive human populations, would have become one vast amplification zone. From the cities, an altogether more perilous gyre would have surged and widened, diffusing into every crack and crevice of town and village, to become a single pullulating universal wave. Human immunity would have proved no defense against it. Aerosol-spread HIV-1 in about the year 1980 would have proved the ultimate doomsday singularity, the terrifying arrival of a true Virus X.

MISPLACED COMPLACENCY

A self-deluding complacency lies behind our present refusal to come to terms with such a threat. It goes like this: since no such extinction event has ever wiped out humanity in the past, it is impossible that it will happen in the future.

But extrapolating future trends from past history can only be deceiving. In humbling contradiction is the statistic that 99 percent of all of the species that have ever evolved on earth have suffered extinction. The mean survival of a mammalian species is put at about a million years. While suspected causes vary, in fact the fossil record is insufficient to attribute a cause to most of these with any accuracy. But plague infections have been suspected as a possible contributor, possibly a major one, and caused the extinction of at least one species during recent history. Swayne's hartebeest was wiped out by an epidemic of rinderpest, introduced into Africa in the nineteenth century by Indian bullocks used by [the British] army to pull gun carriages.

Past history cannot be a template for the future, for we have altered the earth's ecology on such a scale that a host of unknown major variables have entered the scenario. And, shocking as it might seem, the extinction scenario has actually been tested by the deliberate hand of man. The myxomatosis pandemic in rabbits is now regarded as the classic experiment.

THE RABBIT EPIDEMIC

In 1859 rabbits, a totally alien species, were introduced into Australia as a source of food. Lacking natural predators, their population underwent an explosive expansion, with consequent destruction of grassland and farmland. In 1950, in an attempt to reduce their numbers, wild rabbits in the Murray Valley in southeast Australia were infected with the myxoma virus. This virus, of the genus, *Leporipoxvirus,* lived in a symbiotic relationship with the Brazilian rabbit, *Sylvilagus brasiliensis,* which is a denizen of the tropical forest. The consequences for the Australian rabbits were altogether predictable. The myxoma virus is not spread by aerosol, but as an arbovirus by biting mosquitoes. Nevertheless the prevalence of the vector was so high it became as efficient as a true aerosol spread. Viral "traffic" between the two species began slowly, from May to November, in the rabbits' burrows. Suddenly, in December, the Australian summer, augmented perhaps by a proliferation of the insect vector during a wet spring, the epidemic exploded. Over the course of just three summer months, 99.8 percent of the rabbit population of the entire southeast, a land area equivalent to the whole of Western Europe, became infected and died.

Following this initial annihilation, the tiny surviving population of rabbits began to coevolve with the virus. So, year by year, the mortality fell until, seven years after the introduction of myxomatosis, the lethality was now just 25 percent. Selective changes took place both for more resistant rabbits and for less lethal strains of virus.

At present the AIDS epidemic, which moves much more slowly because of its mode of transmission, may be showing the earliest signs of a similar evolution, as a handful of survivors are being reported. In time, if left to its natural course, even the lethal HIV-1 will evolve, as more and more people survive, until eventually the new human strains of virus coevolve with their human symbiont. After many centuries, the future progeny of HIV-1 may cause no more illness than it currently causes chimpanzees or the Simian immunodeficiency virus (SIV) their host monkeys.

VIRTUAL EXTINCTION

How likely is it that, given the enormous diaspora of viruses in nature, there might already reside one or many species that could, with minimal accommodation, assume the virus X of our worst nightmares?

The human species is essentially a monoculture—comparable in many respects to the rabbits that overpopulated southeastern Australia. The myxomatosis experience, together with the evidence from many past human pandemics, suggests that a percentage of people will be resistant even to the most virulent extinction strain. That resistance derives from the genetic differences that exist between all except identical twins, spread over all of the races and differing populations of people throughout the world and the widely varying ecologies they inhabit.

Total human extinction is therefore unlikely as a result of a viral pandemic, but a near miss, such as the rabbits experienced with myxomatosis, or even a lesser global lethality, would prove so catastrophic socially and psychologically that we can derive only limited comfort from this.

"The only trouble with all this
foaming viral paranoia was that it
had nothing to do with reality."

EMERGING VIRUSES DO NOT THREATEN HUMANITY WITH EXTINCTION

Ed Regis

Ed Regis, a former professor of philosophy, is a science writer whose books include *Who Got Einstein's Office?* and *Great Mambo Chicken and the Transhuman Condition.* The following viewpoint is excerpted from his book *Virus Ground Zero: Stalking the Killer Viruses with the Centers for Disease Control.* Regis argues that the threat viruses pose to humanity has been overstated. Public anxiety over viral outbreaks, he asserts, are ironic in light of the fact that the Centers for Disease Control and Prevention (CDC) has been highly successful in identifying the causes of mysterious illnesses and in controlling outbreaks of disease. He declares that the widely feared African hemorrhagic fever viruses, such as Lassa and Ebola, have killed few people and can be easily stopped from spreading.

As you read, consider the following questions:

1. What has contributed to increased reports of "new" and "emerging" diseases, according to Regis?
2. What were the three leading causes of death in the United States in 1992, as reported by Regis?
3. What prevents the Ebola virus and similar organisms from presenting a major threat to humanity, according to the author?

On May 14, 1993, Merrill Bahe, a Navajo boy aged nineteen and a marathon runner in the peak of health, died suddenly and mysteriously, gasping for breath, while riding in a car barreling through the desert near Gallup, New Mexico, about twenty miles east of Window Rock. . . .

His fiancée . . . had died equally without warning a few days earlier, gulping for air in the same manner. He'd been on his way to her funeral, in fact, when he was taken ill.

A few days after these events, an investigator from the Indian Health Service in Albuquerque, himself a Cherokee Indian, drove out to Bahe's trailer, entered it, and searched the place for clues. . . .

It was the start of an investigation into a series of unexpected and puzzling deaths in the Four Corners region. Twelve people would die with similar symptoms within the next few weeks, many of them Native Americans living within the borders of the Navajo Indian Reservation, an enormous twenty-thousand-square-mile area about twice the size of Massachusetts.

A SPREADING EPIDEMIC

And then the epidemic started spreading. New cases cropped up in Texas, California, Oregon, and elsewhere, and mysteriously, some of the new victims were also Native Americans. . . .

The disease, whatever it was, caused an unnaturally fast decline and fall, and it seemed to have abnormal inclination for Native Americans, as if this truly were some nightmare contagion that for unknown reasons zeroed in upon the American Indian. The Navajo themselves, who regarded untimely deaths as a punishment for bad living, wondered if the illness was not retribution for their having embraced such white man's evils as fast food, MTV, and video games. If so, the cure for what ailed them would not lie within the purview of science. "Western medicine has its limitations," said Navajo president Peterson Zah.

Even so, within three weeks the Centers for Disease Control (CDC) identified the offending microbe as hantavirus and in two more weeks had found the animal reservoir, the deer mouse. Shortly after that they'd put together a set of guidelines for reducing the risk of exposure to the microbe and had published them in *Morbidity and Mortality Weekly Report*, which was routinely sent to public health officials all across the country.

The Four Corners episode proved to be a landmark case for the CDC. The operation ran in record time and went off without a hitch, and the CDC emerged from it looking like a perfectly designed bureaucratic machine successfully doing its job in silence, which in this case it was.

The Irony of Success

The irony was that the CDC's increasing successes identifying pathogens were looked upon as ominous and threatening, as foreshadowing uncontrolled outbreaks of "new" and "emerging" diseases. Most of the microbes and diseases that the CDC dealt with, however, were not "new" by any standard. Certainly Legionnaires' disease was not: it had "emerged" a long time ago, well before the Legionnaires themselves began falling ill in Philadelphia in 1976, before the county health workers started calling in sick in Pontiac, Michigan, in 1968, and before the St. Elizabeth's patients started dying of pneumonia in July of 1965. The affliction, so far as anyone could tell, went well back into the far reaches of disease history, as did the microbes that caused it. "The bacterium was new only in the sense that it was unfamiliar to laboratory workers," said Joe McDade of the *Legionella* microbe. "The identical bacterium had been isolated in 1947 from a guinea pig inoculated with blood from a patient who had a febrile respiratory illness."

Prior cases of the disease were hard to prove mainly because of the lack of earlier blood or tissue samples that could be submitted to tests. Later cases, however, appeared like clockwork, and soon Legionnaires' disease was "emerging" all over the world.

It was "emerging," however, only in the sense that the disease detectives now had the rapid diagnostic tests, plus lab techniques, instruments, and vast storehouses of reagents, that permitted them to recognize it easily enough when and where it occurred. The availability of these standardized tests, and the tremendous diagnostic power represented by the store of reagents, contributed to the false impression that new diseases were springing up all over the world, like shopping centers, whereas in reality the main thing that was new was the ease and speed with which these diseases could now be identified.

The hantaviruses, for example, were an ancient species of microbe, some of which were thought to have caused outbreaks as far back as A.D. 960. The name itself—originally "Hantaan virus"—was relatively new, coined in 1978 for an outbreak near the Hantaan River in Korea in which 121 American soldiers died among the 2,000 who were stationed in the area. There had been several earlier epidemics of closely related diseases, however, including one in Sweden in 1934, and others in the Soviet Union between 1913 and 1935. The syndrome was common in northwestern Europe, and between 1977 and 1995 some 505 cases had been recorded in northeastern France alone.

"What are commonly termed emerging pathogens are not

really new," said Bernard Le Guenno, a Pasteur Institute virologist. "What appear to be novel viruses are generally viruses that have existed for millions of years."

The rise of "emerging diseases," therefore, was largely an illusion fostered by CDC's own rapidly increasing success at unraveling previously unsolved medical mysteries and discovering previously undetected microbial crimes. The irony of it all was that the better the CDC got at identifying the pathogens that caused age-old but hitherto unrecognized diseases, the more it looked as if scads of trailblazing new microbes were out there amassing themselves for attack, gathering their forces, and preparing to bring us "the coming plague."

The more successful the CDC became, in other words, the more diseased the world looked.

But it wasn't. By almost every measure, the world's peoples were getting steadily healthier: average life expectancy was on the increase, worldwide, among all races; infant and child mortality rates were consistently declining, in both developed and developing countries; the world's population routinely grew, and indeed it had grown fastest in Africa itself, for at least the last twenty years. Outbreaks of health, however, were not considered "news."...

In 1900, the three leading causes of death in the United States were tuberculosis, pneumonia, and diarrheal enteritis—all three of them infectious diseases. By 1992, the three leading causes of death were heart disease, cancer, and stroke—none of them infectious diseases. Infectious diseases, including AIDS, at that point caused only 5 percent of all deaths; one of the biggest national health problems in the 1990s, indeed, was obesity.

"NEW" DISEASES KILL FEWER PEOPLE

Further, the "new" infectious diseases—hantavirus, Legionnaires', and Lyme disease, for example—did not remotely begin to approach the "old" ones in terms of the numbers of people they killed. During the 1918 influenza crisis, half a million Americans had died; hantavirus, by contrast, was known to have affected a total of 133 people in the United States and to have killed 66, starting from the original Four Corners outbreak in 1993.

Except for influenza and AIDS, the country no longer had epidemics, it had outbreaks. But even AIDS, the new scourge, was nothing like the major killers of past history.

"AIDS is what we principally have on our minds at the moment," said disease historian William McNeill at Stephen Morse's landmark Emerging Viruses conference in 1989. "But I must say that it is a poor country cousin in terms of the slowness of its propagation and the obviousness of behavioral adjustments that would check its spread. . . . It is always worth reminding oneself that more people die of automobile accidents each year than—I think it is still correct to say—have yet died of AIDS in the United States. Demographically, in terms of its effect on population, it is not yet a major phenomenon."

WE CAN PREVENT FUTURE PLAGUES

Many people, biologists among them, have suggested that our species is headed for a drastic Malthusian solution to the growing problems of population growth and ecological damage. We are so crowded, and have damaged our environment so much, that surely some new plague or plagues will sweep through the planet, decimating our species. It will fall to those of us who survive to rebuild the shattered remnants of civilization and (perhaps) learn the perils of reproducing too quickly and damaging the environment too much. Such a dramatic reduction in population, accompanied by great societal changes, took place in Europe during the Plague of Justinian and later during the Black Death. Why shouldn't a similar disaster happen today?

I am confident that no terrible disease will appear that slaughters us by the billion. The reason is that we can now respond very quickly to such a visible enemy. Any disease that spreads like wildfire will have to do so through the air or the water, and there are many steps we can take right away to prevent such a spread. If the people of fourteenth-century Europe had known what we know now, they could have halted the Black Death in short order.

Christopher Wills, *Yellow Fever, Black Goddess*, 1996.

Five years later, by 1994, total cumulative U.S. AIDS deaths were 270,533; in that same year, however, 32,330 people died of AIDS while 43,000 died in traffic accidents. Still, the spread of AIDS could be, and in fact had been, curtailed by "behavioral adjustments," and this was a disease in which human behavior, as much as the virus itself, played a major role. . . .

THE MEANING OF THE 1995 EBOLA OUTBREAK

What was the significance, if any, insofar as public health was concerned, of the 1995 Ebola virus outbreak in Kikwit [a town in the Democratic Republic of the Congo, formerly Zaire]? Some public health officials, at the beginning, had made some fairly rash pronouncements, especially those on the order of

"This is the big one," which turned out to be just a wee bit of an overstatement. Even Bill Clinton had used some fateful terms when, in a June 26, 1995, speech commemorating the fiftieth birthday of the United Nations, he spoke of "fatal diseases like the Ebola virus that could have threatened an entire continent."

An entire continent? Well, maybe. But the truth was that these and other such apocalyptic claims were tokens of an emerging new paradigm concerning the fundamental meaning of disease as well as its ultimate cause, the microbes. Disease, according to this new view, was not merely an artifact of biodiversity, a by-product of our sharing the planet with lots of other life-forms including rickettsias, bacteria, and viruses. No. Disease was, instead, an independent power, a corrective force, a moralistic and vengeful influence. It was nature's way of defending itself against invasive and unsightly humans.

This was the viewpoint that had been expressed by Richard Preston in The Hot Zone: "In a sense, the earth is mounting an immune response against the human species," he'd said. "Perhaps the biosphere does not 'like' the idea of five billion humans. . . . The earth's immune system, so to speak, has recognized the presence of the human species and is starting to kick in. The earth is attempting to rid itself of an infection by the human parasite."

Not only was it attempting to do so, it was actually succeeding in the attempt, at least according to Laurie Garrett in The Coming Plague: "That humanity had grossly underestimated the microbes was no longer, as the world approached the twenty-first century, a matter of doubt," she said. "The microbes were winning." (How it could be that the microbes were "winning" when the average life expectancy of the world's population steadily increased, when childhood mortality rates steadily decreased, when the global population spiraled forever upward, and when Africa, home of the world's most lethal viruses, had the world's highest rate of population growth year after year, was a mystery. It was during the years of the Black Plague, when the world's population actually declined, that the microbes were "winning.")

A New View of Nature

So radical and sweeping was this new paradigm that it represented a revised conception of nature itself. Nature, not so very long ago, had been regularly portrayed as "fragile." This was the conventional wisdom, it was the orthodox, established, and canonical view. The ecosystem, supposedly, was in a condition of such delicate equipoise that the slightest perturbation could wreak havoc and ruin everything. That was why nature had to be conserved, saved, and protected, after all, because nature was so very "fragile."

Well, nature was fragile no longer. Somehow, it had rallied. It had rebounded, snapped back, and gathered together its strength, to the point that the same natural world that formerly had to be protected from humanity had suddenly become humankind's chief exterminator. Far from being fragile, nature was now almighty and vindictive. And it was highly intolerant of its very own creation, people.

As were the microbes themselves. All at once viruses had replaced the A-bomb as the object of the apocalyptic vision. No more would doomsday appear in the form of ballistic missiles raining death from out of the clouds; instead, destruction would rise up out of the rain forests in an act of viral correction and punishment. "AIDS is the revenge of the rain forest," Preston had written. "It is only the first act of the revenge."

So when Ebola once again crawled out of the primeval jungle and started killing people in Kikwit, what could it be but the fulfillment of a prophecy, the final act in the unfolding drama? What could it mean but that The End was Nigh?

Who could blame the public, then, when an Internet discussion group was created under the title "The Ebola virus—the end of the civilized world?" and people began saying things like:

> That the Ebola virus is a terrible threat to mankind is undoubtable, but I wonder if anybody has thought about the consequences of an epidemic disaster in areas with high concentration of population—for example central Europe or the eastern coast of the USA.

> Ebola kills 88 percent of the victims, and thus would such a populated area be reduced to almost nothing. . . .

> Indeed, Ebola is the mightiest threat mankind has faced yet.

And so on.

THE STUFF OF LEGEND AND HOLLYWOOD

The only trouble with all this foaming viral paranoia was that it had nothing to do with reality. It was, instead, the stuff of legend. It was Hollywood, it was the movies, it was box office.

Indeed it was worse than that. The "revenge of the rain forest" doctrine was in fact a return to a prescientific, animistic conception of nature: it was a throwback to the days when the gods were portrayed as stomping about in heaven and hurling thunderbolts down from the sky. The only difference was that these days they were slinging viruses.

The world's virologists themselves soon rose up against the oncoming tide of virus paranoia, and it was symbolically fitting that some of the most vocal among them were located in Africa, the very place where the fabled viruses hailed from. Margaretha Isaäcson, the South African physician who'd stopped the transmission of Ebola virus at Ngaliema Hospital in Kinshasa during the original 1976 outbreak, said:

> Ebola is of absolutely no danger to the world at large. It is a dangerous virus, but it's relatively rare and quite easily contained.

> The virus needs the right conditions to multiply, whatever the virus is, be it Ebola or plague. It's not enough to just have the accident. The virus must first find itself in a favorable environment before it can affect anyone. The media is scaring the world out of its wits, and movies like Outbreak are doing people a great disservice.

Ed Rybicki, a virologist at the University of Cape Town, said:

> The town of Kikwit has a population of five hundred thousand and extremely poor medical treatment centers, and yet only three hundred people died there. That is not anywhere near 90 percent of the entire population.

> A simple yet very obvious statement of the facts. So if 499,700 people in Kikwit DIDN'T get Ebola, why are Americans so worried????

Indeed. The fact of the matter was that Ebola hemorrhagic fever, along with Marburg and Lassa, were diseases of poverty and bad hospitals. Although they thrived momentarily when they erupted in such environments, those same viruses were stopped cold every time they turned up in well-equipped medical institutions, whether in developed countries or elsewhere. When Marburg, the first of the unholy trio, showed up in Germany in 1967, it infected one round of twenty-five people, seven of whom died, then spread to six secondary cases among medical personnel and family members, all of whom lived. And that was the end of the Marburg epidemic.

The original Marburg incident was, and would remain, the largest human outbreak of any African hemorrhagic fever ever to appear in the developed West, and the virus had killed just seven people. Both Lassa and Ebola, the two other African hemorrhagic fever viruses, would arrive in Europe and the United States on several later occasions, but in none of those instances was there more than a single death, and in no case was there person-to-person transmission of the virus. When in 1969 Penny Pinneo was brought to the Columbia Presbyterian Medical Center New York with Lassa fever, there were no cases of secondary transmission. In 1976, when Geoffrey Platt contracted Ebola in a London lab, the infection started and ended with him. When Lassa was brought into a suburban Chicago hospital in 1989, it got no farther than the first case. And in 1994 when a Swiss primate researcher with Ebola hemorrhagic fever was admitted to the University Hospital of Basel, the patient recovered and the infection stopped then and there.

DEAD CHEMICALS

All of which suggested that these African hemorrhagic fever viruses were something less than omnipotent agents hell-bent on wiping out humankind. They were, in fact, dead chemicals. They were physical entities, particles of matter that, clever as they were on the molecular level and whatever neat tricks of information coding they were capable of, still had to obey all the normal laws of chemistry and physics. They still had to get from one person to the next before they could do further damage, and they could be prevented from doing so by the placement of simple physical barriers between them. Common and ordinary items such as rubber gloves, plastic gowns, and face masks could halt an epidemic. A killer virus could itself be killed by a liberal application of household bleach. Precisely those items, mundane and boring as they were, had been the very things that had terminated the Ebola outbreak in Kikwit.

Bernard Le Guenno, after he got back to Paris from Zaire, was invited to speak to scientific groups to tell about his findings and experiences in Kikwit. When he gave his talks, he'd illustrate his comments with a slide show, with pictures of the hospital and the city, plus charts and graphs showing the epidemic curve of the outbreak, the various lines of transmission, and so on. He'd project these images up on the screen to reinforce the different points he wanted to make.

Toward the very end of his talk he showed a slide on which appeared, in French, the single question: "Ebola virus infection— a menace to humanity?"

The next slide in sequence showed only one word: "Non!"

PERIODICAL BIBLIOGRAPHY

The following articles have been selected to supplement the diverse views presented in this chapter. Addresses are provided for periodicals not indexed in the *Readers' Guide to Periodical Literature*, the *Alternative Press Index*, the *Social Sciences Index*, or the *Index to Legal Periodicals and Books*.

Amy Barrett	"War Against the Microbes," *Business Week*, April 6, 1998.
Economist	"Resisting Resistance," May 31, 1997.
Michael Fumento	"Chicken Little Gets the Flu," *Wall Street Journal*, January 14, 1998.
Richard Horton	"Infection: The Global Threat," *New York Review of Books*, April 6, 1995.
JAMA	"Emerging Infections on Center Stage at First Major International Meeting," April 8, 1998. Available from 515 N. State St., Chicago, IL 60610.
Robert W. Lee	"Scaring Us Toward Global Government," *New American*, November 24, 1997. Available from 770 Westhill Blvd., Appleton, WI 54914.
Anne Platt McGinn	"Confronting Infectious Diseases," *Society*, May/June 1998.
David Murray and Joel Schwartz	"Alarmism Is an Infectious Disease," *Society*, May/June 1997.
Hiroshi Nakajima	"Let's Work Together to Control Infectious Diseases," *World Health*, January/February 1997.
Lori Oliwenstein	"Dr. Darwin," *Discover*, October 1995.
Margie Patlak	"Book Reopened on Infectious Diseases," *FDA Consumer*, April 1996.
Jonathan A. Patz et. al.	"Global Climate Change and Emerging Infectious Diseases," *JAMA*, January 17, 1996.
Robert W. Pinner et. al.	"Trends in Infectious Diseases Mortality in the United States," *JAMA*, January 17, 1996.
Dennis Pirages	"Microsecurity: Disease Organisms and Human Well-Being," *Current*, January 1996.
Hanna Rosin	"Don't Touch This," *New Republic*, November 10, 1997.
Ellen Ruppel Shell	"Resurgence of a Deadly Disease," *Atlantic Monthly*, August 1997.
Traci Watson	"Hospital Superbugs: Physician, Wash Thyself, and Other Medical Safety Tips," *U.S. News & World Report*, February 17, 1997.
Brian R. Wolff	"Outbreak of Fear," *Newsweek*, May 22, 1995.

CHAPTER 2

WHAT CAN BE DONE TO CURTAIL THE AIDS EPIDEMIC?

CHAPTER PREFACE

Between 1981 and 1996, between 750,000 and 1 million Americans were diagnosed with acquired immunodeficiency syndrome (AIDS). These people suffered from a weakened immune system, believed to be caused by the human immunodeficiency virus (HIV), which left them vulnerable to opportunistic infections. The virus is primarily spread through sexual contact or through the sharing of needles among drug users. Despite recent promising advances in drug therapy, AIDS remains the leading cause of death of Americans between the ages of twenty-five and forty-four. HIV infection rates are rising among women, blacks, and Hispanics, as well as in some populations in Africa and Asia where few can afford expensive drug treatments. The World Health Organization (WHO) estimates that by the beginning of the twenty-first century, 40 million people worldwide may have become infected with HIV.

Some people have argued that the same methods used for other communicable diseases should be used against AIDS. These options include routine testing for the disease, reporting those infected to public health authorities, and tracking down and informing people who may have been exposed to the disease. Although some states have instituted some of these steps, these public health measures have often not been used in the case of AIDS because of objections that they violate patients' rights to privacy. Advocates of routine testing and reporting maintain that such concerns are misguided and have resulted in people dying needlessly of AIDS. "I have no doubt," states Dr. Frank Judson of Denver's Public Health Department, "that lots of people have become infected and lost their lives as a result of these irrational policies we've chosen to follow."

Many doctors and AIDS activists, however, defend such "AIDS exceptionalism" in public health policy because people at risk for AIDS have legitimate fears of being stigmatized and of losing jobs, insurance, and housing because they are gay or sick with AIDS. They argue that mandatory reporting laws, for example, would cause many people to forgo testing and thus prevent them from receiving counseling and treatment. Testing for HIV, they conclude, should continue to be done on a voluntary and anonymous basis.

The question of voluntary vs. mandatory AIDS testing and reporting is one of several controversies surrounding AIDS and public health policy. The following viewpoints discuss various methods for slowing or stopping the spread of HIV/AIDS.

"Nearly everyone who becomes
infected today could have been saved
if the government had relied on
standard public-health policies used
to curtail other diseases."

TRADITIONAL PUBLIC HEALTH
MEASURES ARE NEEDED TO CONTROL
THE AIDS EPIDEMIC

Tom Coburn

Tom Coburn, an Oklahoma physician, was elected to the House
of Representatives as a Republican in 1994. In the following
viewpoint, he argues that AIDS has continued to spread in the
United States because standard public health measures—such as
routine testing, reporting names of infected individuals to public
health departments, and notifying sexual partners of HIV-infected
individuals—have not been used. Coburn contends that although
these methods have been used successfully against other sexually
transmitted diseases, political pressures have prevented their uti-
lization against AIDS. He describes legislation he introduced in
1997 that would implement some of these public health policies,
such as mandatory disclosure of HIV-positive tests to state public
health departments. Such measures would help prevent the further spread of AIDS and enable HIV-positive individuals to begin
potentially lifesaving medical treatment, he concludes.

As you read, consider the following questions:

1. How many Americans might be unaware that they are
   infected with HIV, according to Coburn?
2. What steps does the author recommend for safeguarding the
   confidentiality of AIDS patients?

In the short period since the first cases of the disease were rec-ognized in 1981, more than 350,000 Americans have died of AIDS. As of 1997, nearly 1 million individuals in the United States are believed to be infected with HIV, the virus that causes AIDS. More than 40,000 new infections are estimated to occur each year. Clearly, this is an epidemic of historic proportions that is out of control.

CIVIL RIGHTS VS. PUBLIC HEALTH

In many ways, the response by the federal government and the public-health community has contributed to the growth of the epidemic. From the onset of the disease, proven medical and public-health practices that were successful in helping to curtail other contagious diseases were abandoned in favor of political correctness. It was decided that HIV would be treated as a civil-rights issue instead of a public-health crisis. As a result, our re-sponse has been based almost exclusively on the rights of those infected to the detriment of the uninfected.

A test to detect HIV has been available for more than a decade, but the medical community has been forbidden to use it for routine testing. This is the result of an agreement made when the Food and Drug Administration, or FDA, approved the test in 1985. Under the guise of privacy, the agency gave in to pressure from gay-rights organizations and limited the routine use of the test for screening by blood banks. Therefore, in the course of a physical examination, a doctor is prohibited from conducting a routine HIV test. No other disease is given protec-tion against diagnosis.

AIDS activists also convinced lawmakers that any form of nonconsensual testing is a civil-rights violation. Because of this, our laws have prevented sexual-assault victims from the right to learn the HIV status of their attackers, even though studies have indicated that treatment immediately following HIV exposure significantly can reduce the chance of infection. According to the AIDS Action Council, which claims to be the nation's leading AIDS-advocacy organization, "Rape and sexual-assault survivors need to take care of themselves and not concentrate on the HIV status of their assailants."

A NONTRADITIONAL APPROACH

In short, our national AIDS/HIV policy relies solely on individu-als submitting to voluntary testing and, if infected, taking the necessary steps themselves to prevent others from becoming in-fected. Never before in medical history have we given the responsibility of controlling an epidemic to the individuals infected with the disease.

This nontraditional approach has put the public's health at risk and done nothing to curtail the epidemic. The fact that half of the nearly 1 million people believed to be infected with HIV in the United States are unaware of their status is proof enough that our AIDS/HIV policies have failed. As a result of this failure, hundreds of thousands are being denied medical care and unintentionally and unknowingly infecting others.

While no cure exists for HIV infection, we do know enough about the virus to prevent its spread, but we have failed to do so. I have introduced legislation—the HIV Prevention Act—which would implement the public-health practices that have been successful in helping curtail the spread of other infectious diseases. These include both disease reporting and partner notification. [The HIV Prevention Act was not passed by Congress as of May 1998.]

WHY REPORTING IS NECESSARY

Reporting is necessary so scientists may study and assess diseases. It enables those responsible for disease control to determine more accurately the extent of an epidemic, rates of progression, direction of spread, possible changes in transmissibility and other critical factors of disease control. This information allows for the development of long-term strategies based on reliable data and the development of effective and targeted prevention-education messages. Currently, more than 50 diseases, including AIDS, are reported to the Centers for Disease Control and Prevention, or CDC.

Because we have based our assumptions on AIDS—the latter stage of the disease—rather than HIV infection, our nation has been unable adequately to deal with the epidemic. AIDS, after all, tends to develop up to 10 years or more after HIV infection. Therefore, unless we change our focus, we never will discover the extent of the epidemic or effectively understand and limit its spread.

Partner notification also is vitally important, because it is the only timely way to alert those in danger of infection. It essentially requires two steps. The first is to counsel all infected individuals about the importance of notifying their partners that they may have been exposed. The second is for their doctor to forward the names of any partners named by the infected person to the Department of Health, where trained public-health professionals complete the notification. In all cases, the privacy of the infected is protected by withholding the name of the infected person from those being notified.

EARLY DIAGNOSIS IS CRUCIAL

The latest therapies available make notification and early diagnosis more crucial than ever. Many of the world's top scientists believe that it may be possible to transform HIV from a terminal illness into a chronic, manageable disease such as diabetes. However, the success of these drugs depends upon starting treatment early. Sadly, most of those infected do not know that they are infected until they become sick with AIDS. By this point they have been denied the medical care that could have prolonged their lives and they may have unknowingly infected others.

Who could deny those who may have been unknowingly exposed to HIV the right to know that they may be infected when such therapies are available? If we were discussing the ebola virus instead of HIV, would those against public-health practices still oppose reporting and partner notification?

AIDS activists incorrectly argue that these practices are counterproductive because they may frighten those at risk from getting tested and drive those who are infected underground. The fact is that no evidence in any of the states with partner notification or HIV reporting exists to support this claim. North Carolina, for example, just recently eliminated anonymous testing, and HIV testing increased by 45 percent.

These same arguments were used against screening blood-bank donors, military personnel, Job Corps and foreign-service applicants and never have proved true.

MANDATORY INFANT TESTING IN NEW YORK

New York's 1996 "baby-AIDS" law is the most recent example of this fallacy being disproved and the effectiveness of traditional health policies being proved. Enacted after studies showed the rate of perinatal HIV transmission could be reduced by two-thirds if the drug AZT is administered, this law requires HIV testing of all newborns. In the program's first three months, the state has more than doubled the number of infected and at risk children identified. These babies and their mothers now receive the medical treatment that they otherwise would have been denied. The babies may be saved from infection and the mothers can take precautions to avoid infecting others. All now will have the opportunity to live longer, healthier lives. State health officials have said that they have received no complaints from mothers or hospitals and that the program is going extremely well.

AIDS activists, civil libertarians and feminist organizations fought this proposal both at the state and federal levels claiming it would scare pregnant women away from receiving care and do nothing to help women or their children. They were wrong. They also are wrong about HIV reporting and partner notification.

THE AIDS EXCEPTION

Since the turn of the century . . . standard public-health measures have been deployed against infectious diseases. These measures, leaving aside the extreme step of holding people in quarantine, have typically included at least some of the following: *routine testing* for infection, often undertaken without explicit patient consent; *reporting* to local health authorities of the names of those who test positive for infection; *contact tracing,* or the identification of any people who may have been exposed to infection; and *notification* of these possibly infected people that they may have been exposed. Some combination of these four practices has been commonly applied against outbreaks of infectious diseases, including typhoid, diphtheria, and tuberculosis, and against upsurges in sexually transmitted diseases. It would be surprising if, out of all the viruses and bacteria that can do us significant harm, one was exempted from the scope of these measures. It would be even more surprising if the one chosen pathogen was responsible for an epidemic that today constitutes the leading cause of death among all Americans aged twenty-five to forty-four.

This very thing has, of course, happened, largely in order to accommodate civil-rights concerns. The practice of traditional public health has been to a great degree suspended for acquired immune deficiency syndrome and for human immunodeficiency virus, the virus that causes it. Although various traditional public-health steps are being taken against AIDS and HIV, in differing combinations from state to state, the result is a chaotic patchwork—one that is inadequate, a growing number of critics say, to the task of containing and eradicating AIDS.

Chandler Burr, *Atlantic Monthly*, June 1997.

With the success of baby AIDS in New York and similar programs elsewhere, I am confident that we eventually will embrace traditional health measures. We already are moving in that direction. A majority of states have HIV-reporting and partner-notification laws. The American Medical Association has declared its "strong support" for the provisions of the HIV Prevention Act. I expect that the CDC also will become more vocal in supporting similar efforts. Even civil libertarians such as Democratic Sen. Ted Kennedy of Massachusetts have advocated reporting and partner-notification programs. In 1990, Kennedy proposed his own partner-notification legislation, stating that "there is a duty to warn."

CONFIDENTIALITY SAFEGUARDS

Because of the stigma associated with HIV, those with the disease do have legitimate concerns about discrimination. However, herpes, syphilis, gonorrhea, tuberculosis and other contagious diseases have carried stigmas. That is why every state has strict confidentiality laws in place for all medical records. Most states even have enacted specific laws to protect HIV-status information. The Americans With Disabilities Act ensures additional protections against unfair treatment toward those with HIV

While these laws alone cannot change widespread, attitudes those with HIV can look to similar efforts, undertaken both today and in the past, for reassurances of their success in curtailing disease and maintaining confidentiality. We also should continue to do what we can to address issues of discrimination and medical privacy, but these are not and never should be obstacles to safeguarding the public health and saving lives.

Others have argued that additional federal funding for HIV education, treatment and research would be more effective than implementing traditional health policies. While I do not disagree that more funding is important, the fact is that AIDS already receives a vastly disproportionate share of the federal budget compared to other diseases. Since 1993, spending for AIDS research has increased by 40 percent, AIDS prevention by 24 percent and AIDS treatment by 173 percent. In 1997 alone, the federal government will spend nearly $8.5 billion on AIDS-related programs. Funding has been, and should rightfully be, a national priority, but we could spend an unlimited amount of money and still never find a cure or vaccine.

SAVING LIVES

As someone who has cared for AIDS patients, I want to do everything that can be done to prevent one more person from becoming infected with this horrible disease. The means to this end are available. Throughout history, epidemics have been stopped by identifying the infected, notifying those exposed, guaranteeing access to treatment and educating those who are infected about how to prevent transmissions. This should have been our AIDS/HIV policy from the onset. Because it was not, thousands of men, women and children have become infected, suffered and needlessly died for some privacy interest. Every day the government spends hiding behind this shroud of privacy and delaying public-health measures, we allow the disease to claim more victims.

Remember, nearly everyone who becomes infected today could have been saved if the government had relied on standard public-health policies used to curtail other diseases. If enacted, the HIV Prevention Act would do just that. It is not a cure for HIV, but along with new drug treatments, it may be our best hope against the disease until a cure is found.

| "AIDS exceptionalism has been an important and necessary doctrine for promoting public health in the face of the epidemic."

THE AIDS EPIDEMIC REQUIRES UNIQUE PUBLIC HEALTH MEASURES

Mark S. Senak

Some people have argued that AIDS has continued to spread in the United States due to society's failure to use traditional public health measures. In the following two-part viewpoint, Mark S. Senak contends that such "AIDS exceptionalism" in public health policy is justified because AIDS is a unique disease. For example, he argues, if the names of individuals who test positive for the human immunodeficiency virus (HIV) were reported to public health departments, many people would refuse to be tested for HIV because of the stigma and discrimination they might face. Changing AIDS policies to include such procedures as routine testing and names reporting should be attempted only if confidentiality can be assured and if all people who test positive for HIV have ready access to drug therapies, he concludes. Senak directs the public policy division of AIDS Project Los Angeles. His writings include the book *HIV, AIDS, and the Law*.

As you read, consider the following questions:

1. What "ages" does Senak use to describe the evolution of the AIDS epidemic in American society?
2. What three factors make AIDS different from other diseases, according to the author?
3. What opinions does Senak express about Tom Coburn's proposed HIV Prevention Act of 1997?

Reprinted from "Frank Talk About HIV Testing" and "Echoes from the Past: Reconsidering HIV Surveillance Practices," by Mark S. Senak, *Catalyst*, August 1996 and Fall 1997, respectively, by permission of the author.

I

In the early days of the AIDS epidemic, there was no test for HIV, only the onset of a sudden illness, which became known as an opportunistic infection. This signaled the onset of the "dread" disease, as the media so often characterized AIDS. This truly was the Dark Age of the AIDS epidemic, when there was little known about what caused the disease or how to determine if one was infected with HIV.

In 1985, the HIV antibody test was developed for the purpose of screening the nation's blood supply. It was one of three major developments during 1985-87 which changed the way society dealt with AIDS. The test was developed, Rock Hudson died of AIDS, and AZT, the first anti-retroviral, was introduced. Suddenly, we could tell if one had been exposed to the virus; there was greater public awareness of AIDS; and, there was a possible treatment option for those living with HIV. The Dark Age gave way to an Age of Limited Enlightenment.

THE DANGER OF TESTING

When the HIV antibody test was developed, it was somewhat of a panacea. However, with the knowledge that came with the test also came a large degree of danger to those who had been tested. The HIV antibody test was not only a marker for infection, but also a marker for discrimination. . . . A test would not only test for exposure to the virus, but would also be a test of relationships with families, lovers, churches, employers, and insurance companies. During this Age of Limited Enlightenment, HIV-positive people were turned away by family and friends, lost their jobs, had their homes burned, were refused treatment by doctors, and had their medical coverage terminated by insurance companies. In short, the environment for taking an HIV test was not safe.

This led AIDS service organizations such as Gay Men's Health Crisis, the largest and oldest AIDS community-based organization in the nation, and AIDS Project Los Angeles (APLA), the second largest organization, to discourage people from taking an HIV antibody test. Their policy and education departments issued flyers and launched ads telling people "Don't Take the Test." It was reasoned that there was little point to taking a test that would determine one's HIV status when there were no real choices about treatment options, particularly as skepticism about the effectiveness of AZT abounded.

In response, federal and state legislatures enacted laws to make discrimination based on HIV status illegal in order to safeguard the confidentiality of people with HIV. This legislation established a limited degree of safety to the testing environment. At the same time, researchers found better ways to treat opportunistic infections experienced by people with HIV disease, helping them to live longer, better lives. As a result, AIDS community-based organizations were forced to reconsider their positions on HIV testing. Increased protections coupled with the expanded treatment options for both HIV and opportunistic infections meant that taking an HIV test presented individuals with meaningful choices for the first time in the course of the epidemic.

However, because discrimination was still real for people with HIV, most AIDS community-based organizations encouraged people to be tested under protected circumstances, ideally in situations where they could receive anonymous HIV testing and counseling. Through this process, they could get the information they needed while minimizing their exposure to the potential adverse effects of the HIV test.

A Policy Crossroads

Now the community of people who work in the HIV/AIDS field is again at a policy crossroads. We are entering an Age of Information. In December 1995, the Food and Drug Administration approved protease inhibitors, the first in a new class of drugs to combat HIV. This is only the second class of drugs developed to fight HIV since reverse transcriptase drugs like AZT were approved. While the clinical data on the efficacy of protease inhibitors covers a short period of time, it would appear that these drugs given in conjunction with other drugs—in a process called combination therapy—may have a positive impact on the health of those living with HIV disease. This begs the question whether or not HIV antibody testing should be further expanded so that more people can determine their status and, if necessary, seek treatment. From a policy perspective, however, this is only half the question. The other half is that even if HIV testing is made more available, will access to extremely expensive combination therapy be available to all those who are HIV positive?

Considering the testing question first: the development of new and potentially vastly more effective therapies means that AIDS community-based organizations are obligated to redouble their efforts to get people tested. The crux of the matter is not whether to expand testing, but how to expand it.

The sad truth is that legislation protecting people against discrimination and ensuring confidentiality does not mean that discrimination and confidentiality breaches do not occur. One need only consult legal databases and enter the term "HIV" to see a multitude of litigation born from the stigma still presented by HIV disease. This epidemic combines powerful cultural taboos involving sex—particularly homosexual sex—drugs, and death. The insurance industry is not regulated to the point that an individual with an AIDS diagnosis is guaranteed continued health coverage from their insurance. In short, the protective legislation has not succeeded in making the environment for testing markedly safer than it was before. Clearly, the stigma of powerful cultural taboos cannot be eradicated with the enactment of legislation. Therefore, in seeking to expand access to HIV antibody testing, we must take care to ensure that the environment is as safe as possible.

TESTING HAS PROFOUND RAMIFICATIONS

In examining any proposal to expand testing, the HIV/AIDS community must be mindful that the HIV test has pronounced legal, psychological, emotional, and social ramifications. Because so much is at stake when taking an HIV test, the decision to be tested must be left to each individual. The test should never be administered for the convenience of a health care provider.

The term "routinized HIV testing" is often a code word for mandatory testing (i.e., one will be routinely tested for HIV upon entering a hospital or physician's office). There is no compelling argument for HIV testing under such conditions. To curb the HIV epidemic, testing must remain voluntary. However, the idea of offering HIV testing as a matter of routine at appropriate health checkpoints, such as clinics, hospitals, or physicians' offices, is sound. Under current circumstances, most physicians do not discuss the matter of HIV with their patients. Individuals should be presented with information on their testing options (e.g., confidential and anonymous testing). Implementing a policy such as this would be a simple yet significant step in expanding the number of people who test for HIV.

As we enter an Age of Cautious Optimism around new treatment options for those living with HIV disease, the HIV/AIDS community has its work cut out for it. We are a multifaceted community with varying interests but with one common goal. We all want to reduce HIV transmission. This can only be achieved by people knowing their HIV status. We must remain steadfast in our commitment to protecting individuals' right to voluntary HIV testing in a context which best meets their needs. While we encourage people to be tested, we must work to ensure there are adequate resources to care for all those who test positive for HIV, in light of promising yet expensive treatment options. The policy decisions we advance are critical. Therefore, it is of the utmost importance that we attempt to engage in a dialogue and forge solutions to these problems as a community of concerned people.

II

Cries from around the country are reaching a fervent pitch as journalists call for the end to "AIDS exceptionalism," a term coined in the public health field to describe the manner in which the HIV epidemic has been exempted from traditional public health approaches deployed against infectious diseases. This trend is not limited to fringe publications with a predictable political bend but is emerging in mainstream and even progressive periodicals. A June 1997 article by Chandler Burr in the *Atlantic Monthly* calls for the elimination of AIDS exceptionalism and argues that more of the traditional tools of public health need to be used to combat the epidemic.

Although the discussion of AIDS exceptionalism is one that advocates have engaged in over the years, the current debate is taking place in a new environment. The arguments made against AIDS exceptionalism have gained new currency with the advent of protease inhibitors and the success of combination therapy.

Burr outlines a range of standard public health approaches that have been employed to combat infectious diseases in his *Atlantic Monthly* article. They include: routine testing for infection; reporting to local health officers the names of those infected; contract tracing in an effort to identify any one who may have been infected; and notification of those possibly infected that they have been exposed. Burr's central argument is that "the practice of traditional public health had been to a great degree suspended for [AIDS and HIV]," resulting in a "chaotic patchwork" of responses to the epidemic. He further asserts that "It's time to stop granting 'civil rights' to HIV—and confront AIDS with more of the traditional tools of public health."

AIDS Is Different

Over the years, many have asked, "Why should AIDS be treated differently than other diseases?" The answer is fairly obvious—it should be treated differently because it is different. There are three primary reasons this unique public health response to the AIDS epidemic occurred. First, HIV carried a stigma that was unprecedented with any other public health emergency in American history, surpassing yellow fever and polio. Second, because of this stigma, the use of traditional public health approaches to respond to this epidemic ran the risk of creating an environment for testing which would be deemed "unsafe" by those at highest risk for infection. This fear was well-founded considering attempts throughout the nation to implement repressive measures to "control" the spread of HIV, like a proposal to quarantine those with HIV in California in the mid-1980s. Finally, traditional public health approaches were inappropriate to respond to the HIV epidemic in the late 1980s for a very simple reason: while the ability to identify those infected with HIV existed, there were no viable treatment options. In short, if those infected could not be treated, what was the point in identifying them?

THE ACLU's POSITION ON NAME REPORTING

Recently, there have been renewed calls for HIV surveillance, and specifically for reporting the names of all those who test positive for HIV to public health authorities. Proponents of HIV surveillance and name reporting frequently suggest that there is a conflict between the privacy rights of individuals who have or may have HIV and the public health needs of the country, and that individual civil liberties must take a back seat in order to effectively battle the spread of HIV and AIDS.

In the public debate concerning society's response to the AIDS epidemic the American Civil Liberties Union has consistently advocated policies that protect the public health while respecting civil liberties and individual privacy. . . .

The available evidence shows that, *when it comes to reporting the names of people with HIV, there is no conflict between public health and civil liberties.* Instead, the available evidence strongly suggests that public health measures that respect the privacy of individuals testing for HIV are more effective means of fighting the spread of HIV than intrusive measures like name reporting. Specifically, ... the evidence indicates that reporting the names of those who test positive for HIV will set back public health efforts. For this reason, the ACLU opposes name reporting.

American Civil Liberties Union, *HIV Surveillance and Name Reporting: A Public Health Case for Protecting Civil Liberties,* October 1997.

In light of these factors, the conventional wisdom espoused by those who worked most closely with the epidemic was to create an environment in which individuals would feel secure enough to seek voluntary HIV testing and, when necessary (and available), early intervention. The bottom line: AIDS exceptionalism was a strategy designed to foster a "good" public health response to the HIV epidemic and created a new paradigm for doing so.

To date, the overwhelming majority of AIDS advocates believed that AIDS exceptionalism has been an important and necessary doctrine for promoting public health in the face of the epidemic.

There is no question that with the advent and success of new therapies, advocates must question whether or not the circumstances have indeed changed enough to warrant a shift in public policy. Many AIDS service organizations, including APLA's Public Policy Department, are reevaluating their position on a range of public policy issues like HIV reporting, in light of advances made in treating HIV infection. Clearly, the parameters which define AIDS exceptionalism may need to be changed.

CHANGE MUST BE GRADUAL

However, this change must be rational and gradual. Already, there are drastic and shortsighted proposals being put forth to annihilate the unique public health response developed to respond to the HIV epidemic in the United States.

A misguided legislative proposal, the HIV Prevention Act of 1997, sponsored by Rep. Tom Coburn (R-OK), capitalizes on the growing momentum to eliminate AIDS exceptionalism. This proposed legislation is nothing more than a hodgepodge of punitive HIV testing policies, shrouded in public health tenets, that have been rejected by many medical and behavioral scientists throughout the nation. A *Los Angeles Times* editorial characterized the Coburn bill best as legislation that would "needlessly stoke public fears [about HIV]." [The bill remained unpassed as of May 1998.]

As advocates and policy makers debate the role of AIDS exceptionalism in our nation's response to the HIV epidemic, it is imperative that all parties be mindful of two considerations. First, confidentiality protections must be reviewed and reinforced prior to any change in HIV surveillance practices in the United States. While confidentiality laws exist, gaps in protections and variations between states allow significant room for improvement. Second, if leaders demonstrate the political will to implement some form of HIV reporting, then they must also be willing to guarantee that all those infected with HIV will have access to drug therapies once identified. Such a move, asserting a more traditional public health approach to HIV disease and abandoning AIDS exceptionalism—without uniform confidentiality safeguards and access to treatment in place—is nothing more than the injection of politics into a public health equation and, in the end, results in a cruel hoax on those infected with HIV.

"Science's verdict . . . comes down on the side of sanctioning needle exchange programs as an important way of stopping the spread of HIV/AIDS."

NEEDLE EXCHANGE PROGRAMS SHOULD BE ENCOURAGED

Robert E. Stein

One of the ways AIDS is spread is through the sharing of syringes by intravenous drug users. In the following viewpoint, Robert E. Stein argues that needle exchange programs—in which sterile syringes are distributed to drug users—are a highly effective means of preventing the transmission of HIV, the virus that causes AIDS. Moreover, they contend, studies have shown that needle exchange programs do not increase the number of new drug users or the frequency of use by existing users. Stein is vice chair of the ABA AIDS Coordinating Committee, which was established in 1987 to investigate and make recommendations on AIDS-related legal issues to the American Bar Association, a national association for lawyers.

As you read, consider the following questions:

1. What positive effects of needle exchange programs does the author describe?
2. What changes in the law are necessary for needle exchange programs to be effective, according to Stein?

Reprinted from "Sterile Syringes and Needle Exchange Programs: On the Frontline in the Battle to Stop the Spread of HIV," by Robert E. Stein, *Human Rights*, Summer 1997, by permission. Copyright 1997 by the American Bar Association.

Government-approved clean needle programs for substance abusers? At first blush the idea seems counterintuitive for many. Won't this lead to increased substance abuse? Won't it entice nonuser initiates, especially the young? At the very least, won't the government appear to be sanctioning illegal drug using behavior?

Taking into account our society's efforts to reduce illicit drug use, these reactions are expected. However, scientific and public health evidence on this issue has been accumulating for some time, and the answer that the data give to each of the above questions is a resounding "no." Moreover, science's verdict also clearly comes down on the side of sanctioning needle exchange programs as an important way of stopping the spread of HIV/AIDS and other blood-borne diseases.

THE DATA

Needle exchange programs, by increasing the availability of sterile injection equipment, become an important technique in reducing HIV infection among the population of injecting drug users (IDUs) and their often unknowing sexual partners and their children. Extensive studies by the nation's leading public health and scientific agencies, the Centers for Disease Control and Prevention (CDC) and National Research Council (NRC), have shown that needle exchange programs do not increase the frequency of drug use among existing IDUs and do not increase the number of new drug injectors. The conclusions of these studies have been confirmed by a Consensus Panel of the National Institutes of Health.

Moreover, needle exchange programs involving drug counseling and drug treatment program referrals hold the promise of actually reducing drug abuse.

Many citizens are understandably concerned that needle exchange programs might appear to make the government a contributor to drug abuse and such programs might be interpreted as sending a contradictory message about illicit drug usage. However, so long as such programs make available drug counseling and drug treatment referrals, these needle exchange programs should be viewed as a new and different component of government and community efforts to stem the cycle of drug abuse.

Furthermore, because public health policies dictate the use of only sterile syringes, and the evidence is that needle exchange programs result in substantial harm reduction in our communities, on balance they are an important, constructive step. The most rapidly expanding source of new HIV infection is the population of injection drug users, their sexual partners and their children. The only way to protect sexual partners of IDUs and their children from HIV infection (other than abstinence) is by use of sterile syringes.

OTHER POSITIVE EFFECTS

Drug treatment programs should be a component of any needle exchange program because drug treatment programs provide the most effective means of reducing drug dependency. The trust that is developed in community-based needle exchange programs enhances the likelihood of IDUs participating in HIV prevention and counseling, taking advantage of referrals to social and medical services, and actually entering into drug treatment programs.

Unfortunately treatment on demand is not always available due to financial and individual limitations, but needle exchange programs can keep IDUs uninfected until they enter a treatment program.

PREMEDITATED MURDER

Speaking at the XI International Conference on AIDS in Vancouver in July 1996, actress and activist Elizabeth Taylor made headlines when she called the U.S. government's stand on needle distribution "a glaring example of politics and social squeamishness. In a society that claims to value human life above all, the deliberate withholding of the means to self-protection is more than passive neglect. It is a measured act of premeditated murder."

Stephen Arrerdell, POZ, November 1996.

In addition to significant savings of public funds resulting from reduced HIV infection (always important in times of budget constraints), needle exchange programs remove infected needles from playgrounds, streets and trash receptacles, thereby protecting children, sanitation workers and others from needle sticks. Moreover, law enforcement officers, who inevitably come in contact with hypodermic needles while performing narcotic arrests, will benefit from the clean needles distributed through needle exchange programs and the resulting reduction of contaminated needles.

LEGAL BARRIERS

There are now almost one hundred needle exchange programs operating successfully across the United States—most in areas in which legal barriers have been removed. There are many other communities that would institute needle exchange programs but for those legal barriers. Removal of these barriers is also supported by public health organizations and the American Medical Association.

Among the specific legal changes that have been found to be effective in facilitating the establishment of successful needle exchange programs are: exempting needle exchange programs from criminal and public health laws restricting the sale, distribution and possession of drug paraphernalia; repeal of pharmacy laws and regulations to permit purchase of a limited number of sterile syringes without a prescription; and modification of drug paraphernalia laws to remove syringes from the scope of such laws.

That said, the determination of which legal barriers should be removed to permit the effective operation of needle exchange programs should turn on the laws, policies, customs and attitudes of each jurisdiction.

THE GOAL: SAVE LIVES

Clearly, the efforts of substance abuse treatment advocates and HIV/AIDS advocates are directed towards the same goal: saving lives. Substance abuse counseling and treatment save lives by getting users off drugs; needle exchange programs save lives by keeping users free of HIV/AIDS until they are off drugs.

"Even if needle exchange programs do save thousands of lives in the short term, they amount to a morally and socially unacceptable accommodation to drug use."

NEEDLE EXCHANGE PROGRAMS SHOULD NOT BE ENCOURAGED

W. Bradford Wilcox

W. Bradford Wilcox is a doctoral student in sociology at Princeton University and editor of *Regeneration Quarterly: A Forum for Orthodox Engagement*. In the following viewpoint, he expresses his opposition to needle exchange programs (NEPs), in which intravenous drug users are given clean syringes in order to avoid the spread of AIDS through the practice of sharing needles. Such programs, he argues, encourage illegal drug use, provide a false sense of security to both addicts and public health officials, and fail to control the spread of AIDS. Illegal drug users should be given treatment to end their addiction, Wilcox concludes.

As you read, consider the following questions:

1. On what criteria should needle exchange programs be judged, according to Wilcox?
2. According to Wilcox, what responsibilities does the community have with regard to drug abuse?
3. In what three ways will NEPs undercut efforts to discourage drug use, according to the author?

Reprinted from "Morality and Needle Exchange: A Debate: Doing the Devil's Work," by W. Bradford Wilcox, *The Responsive Community*, Summer 1995, by permission of *The Responsive Community*.

Politicians, public health advocates, and AIDS activists have unleashed a new weapon in the war on HIV: needle exchange programs (NEPs). By 1995, proponents had succeeded in overcoming intense opposition from some religious leaders, black leaders, and drug treatment providers to convince 20 major U.S. cities—from Seattle to Boston—to open publicly-funded needle exchanges. The programs, which provide drug addicts with clean needles in the hopes that addicts will refrain from using ones tainted by the deadly virus, are supposed to save thousands of lives by reducing the spread of AIDS among the group that is now experiencing the biggest increase in HIV infection: intravenous drug users, their sexual partners, and their children.

An Unacceptable Accommodation

Even if NEPs do save thousands of lives in the short term, they amount to a morally and socially unacceptable accommodation to drug use. By providing addicts with the instruments of their addiction, NEPs implicate communities in a pathology that destroys addicts and those with whom they live and (sometimes) work. By acquiescing to the inevitability of drug use, NEPs also reduce the effectiveness of social and legal prohibitions against drugs and contribute to a climate of moral indifference. NEPs cannot be judged simply for their impact on public health. They must also be judged by how they affect the public's moral and spiritual well-being.

The apostles of accommodation see no higher good than saving addicts' lives—regardless of the means by which those lives are saved. However, the religious and moral traditions of many Americans suggest that some acts cannot be condoned—no matter how desirable the consequences—because they are intrinsically evil. The question then becomes not whether NEPs are effective, but whether they amount to an accommodation of the evil of drug abuse.

Drug use is a pathological behavior that saps the will and independence of the addict and wreaks havoc on the communities in which addicts live. As Judge Reggie Walton of the Washington, D.C. Superior Court has said, drug use often ends in "child abuse, murder, and the deterioration of community." Too often, our society offers aid and comfort indiscriminate of right behavior. But if we aim to maintain a vital moral climate, we must actively discourage immorality. Communities have a clear responsibility to stand in solidarity with those who have made the right decision—the many men, women, and children who have had the courage to resist drug use in the first place or to confront their addictions and seek treatment. We only silence the moral voice of the community by distributing syringes to addicts.

This is not to say we should abandon them. Leaving addicts to their fate would be just as callous as providing them with the instruments of their addiction. Addicts deserve a measure of our sympathy, but true sympathy means confronting them in a spirit of tough love with the requirement of treatment. True sympathy also means coming up with the necessary treatment dollars.

MORAL DECISIONS

There are those who would suggest that these are simply moral objections to needle exchange and, as such, amount to little consequence for the world we all inhabit. But the moral decisions we make as a community effect our common life together. The social implication of NEPs is that drug use will continue apace and might even rise. Proponents, pointing to the Centers for Disease Control's (CDC) finding that NEPs have not been clearly linked to increases in drug use, dispute this. The CDC, however, did not rely on any sophisticated methodological survey of drug use; it looked only at rough indicators of drug use immediately following the introduction of NEPs in six U.S. cities. Changes in a community's moral climate inevitably take some time to filter into its social life, and therefore have a complicated relationship to behavior. NEPs, should they become fixtures in urban America, will undercut in three ways our ability to instill the kind of fear necessary to get addicts into treatment and keep others off drugs.

THE LUNACY OF NEEDLE EXCHANGE

The needle-exchange lunacy is evidence that our society is losing, not only its moral center of gravity, but also its ability to reason—to think logically and respond rationally to political, social and medical problems.

Joseph Farah, *Los Angeles Times*, January 13, 1997.

First, NEPs will give addicts and potential addicts a sense of physical security about drug use. In the view of the late Richard Herrnstein, a psychiatrist at Harvard University, "Needle exchange undermines the one thing restraining addiction: fear [of AIDS]." Without the fear of AIDS hanging over them, many addicts will avoid confronting the difficult decision they must make to stop shooting up.

Second, needle exchanges also provide public health officials with a sense of security about AIDS that will lead them to forget the drug abuse that causes needle-borne AIDS transmission in the first place. While most NEPs make some effort to refer their clients to treatment, others have an institutional logic that aims merely to sanitize drug use rather than to stop it. For example, Pat Christen, director of the San Francisco AIDS Foundation, told the CDC that needle exchange "should never ever be linked to a demand to go into treatment, that [treatment] should be just an option that is presented and that it should be presented in the most neutral, nonjudgmental fashion possible. And it should be very clear to the [users] that if they never go into treatment they will still have access to the [needle exchange] . . . , that they are really important in our community, and we want them alive and, well, healthy."

Third, NEPs create a climate of complacency in which the public and its leaders can avoid the difficult choices and expenditures required to get a handle on drug pathologies. This course has met with devastating results in countries such as Switzerland and Italy, where authorities have made drug use easier and safer for their citizens and then watched drug use explode. As the Reverend Graylan Ellis-Hagler, who changed his position on NEPs after being implored to do so by ex-addicts in Boston, argues, "Needle exchange is a dodge from the real issue: getting more drug treatment."

ZERO TOLERANCE

Addicts need to be picked up off the streets and confronted with the stark alternative of jail or treatment. In turn, cities and charitable institutions have a responsibility to make sure such treatment is available. But zero tolerance for drug abuse must continue to be our credo, even as we move to meet the spiritual, social, economic, and treatment needs of city residents. As Reverend Ellis-Hagler reminds us, "The true formula for liberation is getting clean and liberating one's community from the ball and chain of addiction."

"Why embark on a huge national venture to create a vaccine for a disease that is already extraordinarily preventable?"

AN AIDS VACCINE IS NOT NECESSARY TO END THE EPIDEMIC

Charles Krauthammer

In May 1997, President Bill Clinton called for the United States to set a national goal of developing a vaccine for AIDS within the next ten years. In the following viewpoint, Charles Krauthammer questions the need for expending the nation's limited resources on such an effort. He argues that AIDS is already easily preventable because it is not spread by casual contact but is instead transmitted through avoidable behaviors: unsafe sexual activity and intravenous drug use. Rather than attempting to produce a vaccine, Krauthammer maintains, public health efforts should concentrate on reducing these behaviors. Developing a vaccine for AIDS, he asserts, should be considered no more important a national priority than developing a vaccine for lung cancer that would enable people to smoke without health risks. Krauthammer is a nationally syndicated columnist.

As you read, consider the following questions:

1. How have people reacted to President Clinton's call for a national effort to develop an AIDS vaccine, according to Krauthammer?
2. What made polio a worthwhile target for vaccine research, in the author's opinion?
3. What public health measures have been used against diseases other than AIDS, according to Krauthammer?

The reviews are in on President Bill Clinton's dramatic declaration on May 18, 1997, pledging the United States to finding an AIDS vaccine, moonshot-like, within 10 years. Apart from AIDS activists who complain that the president did not commit serious moonshot money to the enterprise ("cheap talk"—playwright Larry Kramer), the reaction was mostly favorable. Who, after all, can be against a vaccine against anything?

AN INDELICATE QUESTION

No one seems to want to raise the obvious, if indelicate, question: Why embark on a huge national venture to create a vaccine for a disease that is already extraordinarily preventable?

Unlike most communicable diseases, AIDS is not contracted casually. Unlike tuberculosis, it is not contracted by being coughed on in the subway. Unlike dysentery, it is not contracted by drinking the wrong water. To get AIDS you must, in all but the rarest cases, engage in complex consensual social behavior, namely unsafe sex or intravenous drug abuse.

It would be nice to live in a world where one could engage in such behaviors while enjoying vaccine-induced immunity. But is that really a top national priority? Would any president propose as a top national priority an anti-lung-cancer vaccine so that people who smoke—48 million Americans do—could do so with immunity?

Nor do presidents call for a 10-year campaign to produce a vaccine against cirrhosis of the liver. Why? Not because we want to stigmatize people who drink or smoke. But for a very practical reason: These behaviors being voluntary and preventable, it makes a lot more sense to spend the scarce intellectual, scientific and financial resources of the country trying to give people immunity from diseases that they cannot otherwise protect themselves against.

The classic case is polio. When Franklin D. Roosevelt contracted it in 1921, we had not a clue how people got it. By the 1950s, frightened parents kept their children away from swimming pools and movie theaters and even crowds. They lived in terror not knowing what they might be doing that was contributing to their kids' chances of getting polio.

With no obvious behavioral cause, polio was the classic case of a disease crying out for a vaccine. Meningitis, cervical cancer and multiple sclerosis occupy a similar position today. But AIDS?

TRADITIONAL PUBLIC HEALTH METHODS ABANDONED

Moreover, Clinton is calling for a huge technological innovation (which many in the field doubt is a reasonable prospect anyway) to prevent the spread of AIDS. Yet, at the same time, the traditional way of controlling the spread of communicable diseases has been largely abandoned in the case of AIDS. And uniquely in the case of AIDS.

We fight just about every epidemic—tuberculosis, syphilis, gonorrhea—by identifying carriers and warning their contacts. The usual epidemiological tracing has not been done for AIDS. Gay activists and civil libertarians have vociferously opposed it. And the politicians have caved.

MORE PRESSING CONCERNS

Most scientists are deeply skeptical of the possibility of an HIV vaccine—HIV is a complex, multi-strained retrovirus that's in a constant ferment of mutation, exceedingly difficult to vaccinate against. . . .

It is a laudable goal, but there are many more pressing concerns that Bill Clinton could address.

New Republic, June 9, 1997.

The story of this travesty—"the effective suspension of traditional public health procedures for AIDS"—is laid out in damning detail by Chandler Burr in the June 1997 *Atlantic Monthly* ("The Aids Exception: Privacy vs. Public Health"). "AIDS has been so thoroughly exempted from traditional public health approaches," writes Burr, "that civil libertarians have defeated in court attempts by health authorities to notify the spouses of people who have died of AIDS that their husbands or wives were HIV-infected."

In 1985, in fact, gay activists brought suit to prevent use of the first test for HIV, unless assured the tests would not be used for widespread screening of gays. Even today they oppose the mandatory HIV screening of pregnant women, even though we know that early treatment of the mothers would reduce by 50 to 75 percent the number of kids born with HIV.

WE KNOW HOW TO PREVENT AIDS

"Traditional public health is absolutely effective at controlling infectious disease," says Dr. Lee Reichman, who works with tuberculosis and AIDS patients. "It should have been applied to AIDS from the start, and it wasn't. Long before there was AIDS, there were other sexually transmitted diseases [STDs], and you had partner notification and testing and reporting. This was routine public health at its finest and this is the way STDs were controlled."

Marcia Angell, executive editor of the *New England Journal of Medicine*, is blunter than most: "I have no doubt . . . that if, for example, we screened all expectant mothers, we could prevent AIDS in many cases. And if we traced partners, we would prevent AIDS in many cases. And if we routinely tested in hospitals, we would prevent AIDS in many cases."

And if we had a president with guts, he would be demanding these elementary measures to save people from getting AIDS today—instead of waving a wand and telling scientists to produce for him a magic vaccine 10 years from now.

| "Our entire nation has a stake in making development of an AIDS vaccine a top priority."

AN AIDS VACCINE IS IMPERATIVE TO END THE EPIDEMIC

H.R. Shepherd

H.R. Shepherd is chairman of the Albert B. Sabin Vaccine Foundation, a private organization that promotes advances in vaccines and immunization. The following viewpoint is taken from an article written in response to a column by Charles Krauthammer, who had criticized President Bill Clinton's May 1997 call for a national campaign to find an AIDS vaccine within ten years. Shepherd argues that Clinton was correct in urging such an effort. He asserts that an AIDS vaccine is the only long-term solution for ending the worldwide AIDS epidemic, especially in developing countries. Discovering such a vaccine, he contends, must remain a high moral and economic priority of the United States and the world.

As you read, consider the following questions:

1. How many people contract HIV every year, according to Shepherd?
2. How many children in the United States have died of AIDS, according to the author?
3. What economic impact does Shepherd assert an AIDS vaccine would have?

Reprinted from "World Needs an AIDS Vaccine—and Fast," by H.R. Shepherd, *Newsday*, July 23, 1997, by permission of the author.

B old proposals for action, no matter how sensible, always attract vocal opponents. So it is with President Bill Clinton's May 1997 call for development of an AIDS vaccine within a decade.

By making an AIDS vaccine a national priority, the president followed the advice of leading medical scientists. Max Essex, chairman of the Harvard AIDS Institute, states the case succinctly: "A vaccine is the only long-term solution for the epidemic."

INVALID CRITICISMS

But syndicated columnist Charles Krauthammer denounced Clinton for rallying the nation behind this vital project. "Why embark," he asked in a June 1, 1997, column carried by Newsday, "on a huge national venture to create a vaccine for a disease that is already extraordinarily preventable?" He asserted that traditional public-health measures alone can stop AIDS, so a vaccine is unnecessary. So simple a solution to one of humanity's biggest crises is alluring. But the allure vanishes in the face of facts.

It is precisely because AIDS is not "extraordinarily preventable" by any means available today that we should embark on a national venture to create an AIDS vaccine. Certainly, more aggressive public-health measures, such as routine testing, should be undertaken. They would slow the spread of HIV in industrialized countries. But they would not come close to halting the pandemic, especially in the Third World, where AIDS is most prevalent but public health resources are most meager.

"To get AIDS," Krauthammer wrote, "you must, in all but the rarest cases, engage in very complicated consensual social behavior, namely unsafe sex or intravenous drug abuse." This assertion misses the mark factually, morally and economically.

A MORAL PRIORITY

A vaccine is a moral priority because of the pandemic's staggering toll on humanity. AIDS kills 1 million people annually worldwide. Each year, more than 3 million people acquire HIV. In the United States, it is the leading cause of death of 25- to 44-year-olds, and of women of childbearing age. The number of Americans infected with HIV—one in every 250—is nearly four times greater than the number of polio cases at the height of that epidemic in the 1940s and '50s.

An AIDS vaccine is a moral priority because the virus does not restrict itself to those who engage in risky behavior. Babies are born with HIV, without engaging in any behavior. The World

Health Organization and the United Nations Children's Fund warn that "projections for Zambia and Zimbabwe indicate that AIDS may increase child mortality rates nearly threefold by the year 2010." Children comprise 10 percent of new infections in Thailand. And AIDS preys upon American children. Already it has killed 4,169 children in the United States, and thousands more have the disease.

A GLOBAL EPIDEMIC

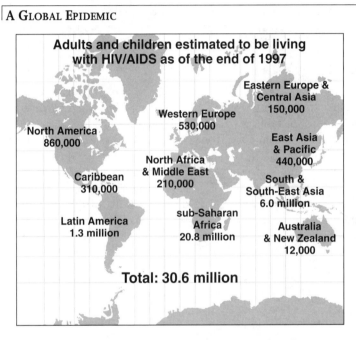

Adults and children estimated to be living with HIV/AIDS as of the end of 1997

North America
860,000

Western Europe
530,000

Eastern Europe &
Central Asia
150,000

East Asia
& Pacific
440,000

Caribbean
310,000

North Africa
& Middle East
210,000

South &
South-East Asia
6.0 million

Latin America
1.3 million

sub-Saharan
Africa
20.8 million

Australia
& New Zealand
12,000

Total: 30.6 million

UNAIDS and WHO Working Group on Global HIV/AIDS and STD Surveillance, *Report on the Global HIV/AIDS Epidemic*, December 1997.

Still, 93 percent of the people with HIV live in developing nations. Ninety percent of AIDS cases worldwide are from heterosexual transmission. Illiteracy and inadequate educational resources make it extremely difficult to teach people in the Third World how HIV is transmitted. Many people simply do not understand that certain behaviors are "irresponsible" and risky.

An AIDS vaccine is a priority because, even if we were able to control the disease here, the virus could be imported. Polio exemplifies this threat. Immunization, combined with strong public-health measures, eradicated polio in the United States in 1979. But American children still must be vaccinated against polio due to the threat of importation.

AN ECONOMIC PRIORITY

An AIDS vaccine is an economic priority. Even people who are indifferent to human suffering must recognize that the United States has direct, economic interests in the rapid development of an AIDS vaccine. The only effective drugs to treat AIDS cost $10,000 to $16,000 per patient, per year. Scientists project each patient will have to take these drugs at least three years, maybe much longer. The lifetime cost to treat one AIDS patient, once estimated at about $120,000, is now rapidly climbing. In contrast, the one-time cost of an HIV vaccine would be $50 to $150 per patient. Immunization against HIV would save the nations tens of billions of dollars each year in treatment costs and lost productivity.

Abroad, as both the number of cases and treatment costs escalate, developing nations cannot possibly afford to care for their AIDS patients. A vaccine would reduce those countries' reliance on economic aid from the United States and other industrialized nations.

One change should be made to Clinton's call to develop a vaccine within a decade. The time frame should be cut in half. The five-year reduction would save billions of dollars and 15 million lives. Our entire nation has a stake in making development of an AIDS vaccine a top priority.

PERIODICAL BIBLIOGRAPHY

The following articles have been selected to supplement the diverse views presented in this chapter. Addresses are provided for periodicals not indexed in the *Readers' Guide to Periodical Literature*, the *Alternative Press Index*, the *Social Sciences Index*, or the *Index to Legal Periodicals and Books*.

Stephen Arrendell	"Panic in Needle Park," POZ, November 1996. Available from 349 W. Twelfth St., New York, NY 10014-1721.
Rick Bluthenthal	"Combating the AIDS Pandemic," *Crossroads*, November 1995.
Ronald L. Braithwaite, Trisha Braithwaite, and Ronald Poulson	"HIV and TB in Prison," *Corrections Today*, April 1998.
Chandler Burr	"The AIDS Exception: Privacy vs. Public Health," *Atlantic Monthly*, June 1997.
Chandler Burr	"Cuba and AIDS," *National Review*, September 29, 1997.
Elizabeth Cross	"Naming Names," *American Medical News*, April 6, 1998. Available from American Medical Association, PO Box 10946, Chicago, IL 60610-0946.
Lawrence O. Gostin and David W. Weffer	"HIV Infection and AIDS in the Public Health and Health Care Systems," *JAMA*, April 8, 1998. Available from 515 N. State St., Chicago, IL 60610.
Dale J. Hu et al.	"The Emerging Genetic Diversity of HIV," *JAMA*, January 17, 1996.
William B. Kaliher	"How Federal and State Policies Spread AIDS," *World & I*, May 1998. Available from 3600 New York Ave. NE, Washington, DC 20002.
Colin Lowry	"The Challenge of Developing an AIDS Vaccine," *Twenty-first Century*, Spring 1998. Available from PO Box 16285, Washington, DC 20041.
Richard Marlink	"Lessons from the March of Dimes," *Harvard AIDS Review*, Spring 1997. Available from Harvard AIDS Institute, 651 Huntington Ave., Boston, MA 02115.
Nancy Pelosi	"Dissent in the House," POZ, July 1997.
Tomas J. Philipson, Richard A. Posner, and John H. Wright	"Government Efforts to Control the Spread of AIDS are Ineffective," *Issues in Science and Technology*, Spring 1994.
Bruce G. Weniger and Max Essex	"Clearing the Way for an AIDS Vaccine," *New York Times*, January 4, 1997.

ARE GOVERNMENT VACCINATION PROGRAMS BENEFICIAL?

Chapter Preface

Vaccines are substances that are injected into the body to stimulate the body's natural immune system against disease. Typically made with dead or weakened (attenuated) forms of the virus or germ that causes the disease, vaccines work by inducing the body to produce antibodies that attack the disease-causing organism.

Most health professionals believe vaccinations are a key to preventing disease epidemics and that maintaining high immunization rates is an important public health goal. Currently most doctors in the United States recommend that all children be vaccinated against several formerly common diseases, including diphtheria, measles, rubella (German measles), meningitis, mumps, polio, tetanus, and whooping cough (pertussis). Many medical organizations also recommend periodical vaccinations for adults. State and federal programs exist that provide vaccinations at low or no cost to poor families. Most states require vaccination before children enter school, but provide exemptions for parents who object for medical, religious, or philosophical reasons.

However, some people have questioned the efficacy and safety of vaccines and have raised objections to rules mandating their use. They argue that vaccinations may cause serious adverse reactions that are worse than the illnesses they are supposed to prevent. Critics also maintain that vaccines often fail to grant lasting immunity to disease and may cause long-term health problems. "The greatest threat of childhood diseases lies in the dangerous and ineffectual efforts made to prevent them through mass immunization," writes doctor and health critic Robert Mendelsohn. The following chapter features different views on vaccination and public health policy.

| "The Vaccines for Children (VFC) program . . . is one important strategy that has helped increase immunization rates."

U.S. GOVERNMENT VACCINATION PROGRAMS HAVE BEEN BENEFICIAL

Children's Defense Fund

In 1993, Congress enacted the Vaccines for Children (VFC) program, in which the federal government purchases vaccines from manufacturers at a set price and makes them available to uninsured and poor children at no cost. In the following viewpoint, taken from a publication of the Children's Defense Fund (CDF), the authors argue that the VFC program and other government and community campaigns have made progress toward the goal of fully immunizing 90 percent of U.S. children by age two. Rising immunization rates have in turn decreased the incidence of vaccine-preventable diseases, the authors assert. The CDF is a private educational and lobbying organization that works on behalf of children.

As you read, consider the following questions:

1. How did childhood immunization rates change between 1992 and 1996, according to the authors?
2. Why is it advantageous, in the authors' view, for children to be able to receive vaccinations from their regular physician rather than from public health clinics?
3. What two proposals did President Bill Clinton make in July 1997 to promote vaccination?

Reprinted from "Child Immunizations Hit All-Time High," *CDF Reports*, October 1997, by permission of the Children's Defense Fund. Copyright 1997, Children's Defense Fund.

The percentage of preschool children in the United States who are protected against certain debilitating and fatal vaccine-preventable diseases has increased to record levels, according to a national survey conducted by the National Center for Health Statistics (NCHS) for the Centers for Disease Control and Prevention (CDC).

RISING VACCINATION RATES

The National Immunization Survey shows that in 1996, 78 percent of 19- to 35-month-old children had all the required vaccinations for measles, mumps, and rubella (MMR); diphtheria, pertussis, and tetanus (DPT); and polio. This compared with 75 percent of 2-year-olds in 1995. A similar survey showed that as recently as 1992 only 55 percent of 2-year-olds were fully immunized. And the immunization rate for toddlers now exceeds 90 percent for such critical vaccines as polio and measles (see Figure 1).

As immunization rates have gone up, the incidence of vaccine-preventable disease have gone down. For example, 47 states and the District of Columbia reported no cases of diphtheria in 1996. Between 1989 and 1995, the incidence of *Haemophilus influenzae*—the leading cause of bacterial meningitis—decreased by 99 percent for children under age 5. In 1996, the CDC reported that tetanus for children under age 15 and polio had been completely eliminated.

"This is very exciting," says Children's Defense Fund (CDF) Health Director Stan Dorn. "Over the past four years [since 1993], more and more preschool children are being protected from preventable childhood diseases. The success we've had at boosting childhood immunizations in recent years is a good example of what we can achieve when all segments of society work together." The public health community, child advocates, parents, the private sector, and federal, state and local governments all deserve credit for this remarkable achievement, says Dorn.

THE VFC PROGRAM

The Vaccines for Children (VFC) program, which Congress enacted in 1993 as part of the Clinton Administration's multi-faceted childhood immunization initiative, is one important strategy that has helped increase immunization rates, according to national experts.

"The VFC program has increased accessibility to immunizations for some of the most neglected children," says Dean Mason, chief of the program support branch for the National Immunization Program at CDC.

VFC makes free vaccines available for uninsured, Medicaid-covered, and Native American children through private doctors and public clinics enrolled in the program. Some children who have private health insurance but whose plans do not cover vaccinations also are benefiting because many states are using their own money, in many instances freed up by VFC funding, to immunize such uninsured children.

FIGURE 1: CHILDHOOD IMMUNIZATIONS

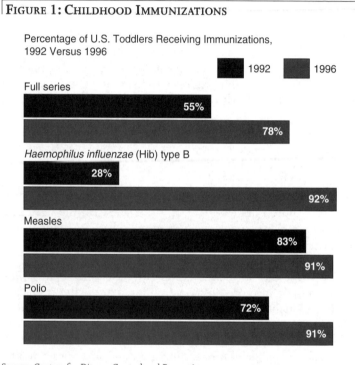

Percentage of U.S. Toddlers Receiving Immunizations, 1992 Versus 1996

■ 1992   ■ 1996

Full series
55%
78%

Haemophilus influenzae (Hib) type B
28%
92%

Measles
83%
91%

Polio
72%
91%

Source: Centers for Disease Control and Prevention.

The goal of VFC is to enable children to receive their immunizations from their regular physician. As of December 1996, 41,845 sites nationally—31,468 of them private—were enrolled in VFC, according to Mason. (The CDC estimates that there are 2.2 providers at each site.) Because vaccine costs had skyrocketed to unaffordable levels for many families with young children, more and more pediatricians—93 percent of those in group practice according to a 1992 *Pediatrics* study—were referring uninsured patients to public health clinics for immunizations even though the children came to their offices for sick visits and check-ups. But short clinic hours, long waiting lists, and the difficulty of making multiple visits for working parents meant that many children were going unimmunized after the referrals.

"Private providers say they no longer feel compelled to refer their patients to public health clinics for reasons of vaccine costs," says Mason, because VFC pays for the vaccine.

A survey of 1,236 pediatricians reported in the September 24, 1997, *Journal of the American Medical Association* found physicians receiving free vaccine supplies are half as likely to make vaccination referrals to public clinics. According to "Impact of Free Vaccine and Insurance Status on Physician Referral of Children to Public Vaccine Clinics," 90 percent of physicians not receiving free vaccine were likely to refer an uninsured child to the health department for vaccination, compared with 44 percent of pediatricians who received free vaccines. In addition, the study found that 77 percent of pediatricians participating in VFC reported a "high level of satisfaction overall" with the program.

Providers like VFC, says Mason, because it helps them provide less fragmented care. "The VFC has increased accessibility by returning children to their medical home," he says.

EFFECTIVE PARTNERSHIPS

In 1995, when only a little over half of New York City preschoolers were fully immunized, child advocates joined forces with the private sector, as well as the city's departments of health, education, transportation, and housing, among others, to spread the word about the importance of early childhood immunization. In 1997, 81 percent of New York City preschoolers are fully vaccinated—a nearly 30 percent increase in just two years.

"We're very happy," says Sandy Trujillo, project coordinator for the Child Vaccination Program (CVP) based in CDF–New York's office. "These stunning results are testimony to all sectors coming together and working toward a common goal."

To remind families that their young children should be immunized, the New York City Department of Health, Chase Manhattan Bank, and CDF–New York developed the Child Vaccination Program, a comprehensive public awareness, community mobilization, and advocacy campaign, in May 1995. Each partner in the campaign—now about 400—helped spread the word by drawing from its own unique resources.

RAISING PUBLIC AWARENESS

Chase Manhattan Bank helped spearhead the public awareness campaign, drawing on its media and publicity resources to help design and launch ads. Through the bank's efforts, the CVP obtained for free more than $2 million worth of advertising, which ran in almost all New York City newspapers and magazines and on most radio and television stations. In addition, Chase gave information about childhood immunizations to its bank patrons through computerized messages on ATM receipts and account statements, and hung posters in its New York City branches. The posters featured baby pictures of celebrities such as Whitney Houston, Jimmy Smits, Danny DeVito, and Spike Lee, with a message emphasizing the importance of children getting all their immunizations.

VACCINES ARE COST-EFFECTIVE

Few measures in public health can compare with the benefits of vaccines. Cost-benefit analyses have been performed for vaccines routinely recommended for children. Four of the vaccines, diphtheria and tetanus toxoids and pertussis vaccine (DTP), measles, mumps, and rubella vaccine (MMR), polio vaccine, and Haemophilus influenzae Type b (Hib) vaccine, accrue direct medical savings for each dollar spent to assure children are immunized against these diseases. Varicella vaccine saves roughly 90 cents in direct medical costs for every dollar invested, while the perinatal and infant hepatitis B vaccination results in savings of 50 cents for every dollar spent. However, when indirect savings are also measured, which includes prevention of work loss by parents to take care of ill children, prevention of death, and prevention of lost earnings from disability, all of the vaccines routinely recommended for children are highly cost saving, ranging as high as $29 saved for every dollar spent on DTP, to $2 saved for the hepatitis B vaccine.

Walter Orenstein, testimony before the Senate Committee on Labor and Human Resources, May 6, 1997.

The New York City Department of Health and the MTA–New York City Transit donated subway and bus space for the posters. The local housing authority distributed information about childhood immunizations to its residents. The New York City Department of Housing Preservation and Development mailed information to its residents in rent bills. And local restaurants, religious groups, schools, child care centers, movie theaters, and grocery stores also displayed posters and distributed information.

Extensive outreach touched 13 city neighborhoods. Representatives from each neighborhood formed a coalition and organized local health fairs and other activities to educate as many families as possible. Advocates also worked to overcome barriers to timely vaccination by educating providers about missed opportunities to vaccinate children and by working to change clinic hours to help working parents and to ensure that clinic staff were bilingual. They also enrolled eligible families in Medicaid and the state's child health insurance program that covers immunizations.

Since the campaign began, calls to the city health department's immunization hotline have increased by 300 to 400 percent, according to Trujillo, and thousands of children have been referred to pediatricians and public health clinics for shots.

"Our goal is to immunize 90 percent of New York City children by the year 2000," says Trujillo. "This goal will be tougher," she says, pointing to new restrictions in the welfare law on immigrant children getting health benefits as one newly created barrier.

MORE WORK TO BE DONE

Continuing to raise children's immunization rates won't be an easy task, advocates acknowledge. They say it will take continued cooperation by all sectors.

"We've done a good job of motivating parents to get their children immunized on time," says Dave Seltz, Immunization Action Plan coordinator at the Ohio Department of Health. Ohio's immunization rates have risen to 79 percent in 1996, from 71 percent in 1995. "It's finding those remaining pockets of need that poses a challenge for us. We need to find a way to keep track of the children who are falling out of the system, such as those children whose parents are moving."

In July 1997, President Bill Clinton unveiled two proposals to help meet his goal of ensuring that 90 percent of 2-year-olds receive all immunizations by the year 2000. One would require parents who receive federal help to pay for child care to have their children immunized, and another would help states set up records systems to track whether children are given vaccines on schedule.

"The recent attention focused on childhood immunizations has been terrific," says Dorn. "To protect our children from disease and keep them healthy, we must keep up the good work."

"The 'Vaccines for Children' (VFC) program ... undermines private-sector investment in new childhood vaccines."

GOVERNMENT VACCINATION PROGRAMS HAMPER THE DEVELOPMENT OF NEW VACCINES

Russell Redenbaugh

The Vaccines for Children (VFC) program is one of several government initiatives designed to provide low-cost vaccinations for poor children. In the following viewpoint, Russell Redenbaugh, a member of the U.S. Commission on Civil Rights and president of a consulting firm, criticizes the VFC program. He argues that by making government the dominant purchaser of vaccines, the VFC program and other government regulations effectively limit their price. The government thus deprives medical and pharmaceutical companies of revenues and removes the incentive to research and develop new vaccines, he maintains. America's failure to improve existing vaccines and to develop new ones could result in disaster for future generations, Redenbaugh concludes.

As you read, consider the following questions:

1. Why are most Americans not terribly concerned about viruses and diseases, according to Redenbaugh?
2. What does the author consider to be a central characteristic of government regulation?
3. What changes in government policy concerning vaccinations does the author recommend?

Reprinted from "Vaccines for Children Program: More Harm Than Good," by Russell Redenbaugh, in *The Dirty Dozen: The Twelve Worse Regulations in America*, edited by John C. Shanahan (Arlington, VA: Alexis de Tocqueville Institution, 1997), by permission of the publisher.

The popular 1994 movie *Outbreak*, starring Dustin Hoffman, helped raise public awareness of the dangers posed by deadly viruses such as Ebola. To Americans living at the precipice of the 21st century, however, such dangers seem far enough removed—and sufficiently unrealistic—as not to worry them.

While viruses such as polio, the measles, mumps, influenza, and rubella used to be life-threatening risks to Americans, they are now largely under control. As a result, the average American born in 1997 can expect to enjoy more than 75 years of life. And, if not, chances are it is because he or she died of something other than a virus such as cancer, heart problems, or a behaviorally-induced cause, such an automobile accident. Even the incidence of AIDS, the most pernicious virus haunting our citizenry, can be dramatically reduced with reasonable life-style precautions.

So it is hard for Americans today to truly fear scenarios such as *Outbreak*. But it may not remain so. Experts warn of a new wave of deadly viruses that may haunt generations of Americans in the 21st century. And the question is: will medical science be prepared to combat these epidemics? And will it be prepared to do so *before* they inflict heavy casualties?

If not, our failure to do so may well be attributed in large part to a law called the "Vaccines for Children" (VFC) program, which undermines private-sector investment in new childhood vaccines.

LOOKING BACKWARD

The nature of regulation is to always look backward—solve the problem that one used to have—and impose a structure that's rigid and unadaptable and decreases the responsiveness of the society, medical community and public health. Regulations always have a cost, and the cost is in the adaptability of the system. This occurs because regulations specify or heavily influence which actions can and can't be taken.

By their nature, regulations specify and generate procedures rather than the "system's" organic ability to respond to new concerns. An approach based on procedures can be sound when the components of the system are incredibly well-behaved and predictable. In the world of Newtonian physics, where forces, interactions and reactions are well understood, this makes sense. But in social and biological systems that involve humans, actions, and viruses, components are neither well-behaved nor predictable.

The law of unintended consequences always shows up when we confuse the well-ordered world of Newton with the messiness of human systems, or more precisely, biological systems. Viruses have one imperative—to survive. They do so by capturing the DNA of the host and forcing a replication of the virus's genetic material.

I can't think of anything more dangerous than to freeze the medical system with regulations that hinder the ability of firms to create and develop new vaccines to combat ever adapting viruses. Yet the Vaccines for Children program does just that.

The program was designed in 1993 as a "single-payer" system for administering childhood vaccines. Despite opposition to a similar system in the health care reform debate, VFC survived largely intact, ironically because it purported to ensure and facilitate the immunization of all children.

According to the *Journal of the American Medical Association* (JAMA), however, by the time children enroll in school, 97 to 98 percent of them already are immunized, even in the inner city. So it was never clear why VFC was needed, other than as a component of President Clinton's overall health care proposal.

In fact, as Robert Goldberg, Ph.D. points out in a 1995 critique of the program, "In its final form, VFC had all the elements of a single-payer health care system, [including] . . . the virtual elimination of a private market for vaccine purchases and delivery . . ." In addition, says Goldberg, the law imposed fee caps on pediatricians and specified that "new vaccine prices would have to be negotiated with the administration."

HAMPERING RESEARCH

Yet, as a 1995 report commissioned by the Department of Health and Human Services (HHS) explains, "private sector sales [of vaccines] make a significantly larger contribution to vaccine industry R&D [research and development], interest, taxes, and earnings [than public sector sales]—ultimately generating the cash flow to fund dividend payments to investors and capital expenditures to support the growth of the business." It notes that since private sector doses sell at a higher price than public sector doses, companies are able to devote more resources to R&D. In fact, each dose sold through the private sector contributes $8.40 to vaccine R&D compared to only $2.90 for public sector sales. In other words, each private sector dose generates almost three times as much R&D as a public sale dose.

Thus, private sales have typically generated hundreds of millions of dollars in revenues which are used to develop new vaccines to combat future health threats to children. But in the absence of a flourishing private-sector market, there is little incentive for companies to invest in new vaccines. Developing new vaccines is a long, costly, and financially risky process. This problem is compounded by the steadily increasing costs of bringing new vaccines to market. The HHS report notes that:

> a vigorous biotech industry is essential to the development of new vaccines, but the funding of biotechs is very fragile, . . . [Moreover], money from venture capitalists is fluid and unsteady; the commitments to provide money are generally short term; and the flow of cash can be turned off quickly if the anticipated returns are not promising.

Markets work by *rewarding* risk-taking and entrepreneurship. This means venture capitalists will not invest in the development of new vaccines if doing so earns them relatively little compared to other investments. VFC is thus destructive of the very reward system that has eliminated the fear of epidemics that plagued prior generations.

A FAILURE TO DEVELOP NEW VACCINES

Ensuring that all American children are fully immunized is important. So, too, is the development of new vaccines that will prevent future epidemics. With a robust vaccine market, these two goals do not conflict. In fact, quite the opposite: they are complementary. Yet, VFC puts development of new vaccines at risk, while as Dr. Goldberg points out, doing virtually nothing to improve immunization levels for American children, which were already very high.

CRITICIZING THE VACCINES FOR CHILDREN PROGRAM

[A July 1994 General Accounting Office] report found that the government was way behind in arranging purchase contracts with the vaccine makers, unprepared to process orders from the doctors intended to receive the vaccine, unprepared to test whether its new delivery system could ensure the potency of the temperature-sensitive vaccines . . . and unable to detect or prevent fraud and abuse. . . .

"It is unlikely that the provision of free vaccines through the VFC will boost coverage in the most affected groups, for whom vaccines are already free, or among other groups when previous experience strongly suggests that this is not an important consideration for the parents. . . . If coverage increases, it may be in spite of the VFC program," the report concluded.

Robert Pollock, *Reason*, November 1994.

Our country's failure to develop new vaccines, by contrast, is a real and present problem. "I would not want to overstate the risk, but clearly we are vulnerable," says Dr. Stephen Morse, a faculty member at Columbia University's School of Public Health and author of *Emerging Viruses*.

The Centers for Disease Control reports that newly developed vaccines provide tangible economic benefits to society between six and 30 times their cost. Yet, HHS points out, "investment in new vaccines is being discouraged" as a result of U.S. government policies. In the midst of this growing problem, the Vaccines for Children (VFC) program has been implemented which is stripping investment incentives further. For the sake of our children and future generations of Americans not yet born, and for the health and well-being of us all, we should eliminate this regulatory program and once again unleash the entrepreneurial spirit and research talents that made us safe from the viral scourges that once ravaged humankind.

"Health authorities . . . assure us of [vaccines'] safety and effectiveness. Yet these seemingly rock-solid assumptions are directly contradicted by government statistics, medical studies, . . . and reputable research scientists."

VACCINES ARE UNSAFE AND INEFFECTIVE

Alan Phillips

Alan Phillips is the director of Citizens for Healthcare Freedom, a nonprofit organization dedicated to empowering individuals to make informed vaccination decisions. In the following viewpoint, taken from his report "Dispelling Vaccine Myths," Phillips argues that vaccines are not safe and effective. They frequently cause adverse reactions, he claims, including death and long-term health problems. Furthermore, he asserts, no real proof exists to demonstrate their effectiveness in preventing disease.

As you read, consider the following questions:

1. What circumstances led Phillips to explore the safety of vaccines?
2. What relationship exists between vaccinations and Sudden Infant Death Syndrome (SIDS), according to the author?
3. How dangerous are most childhood diseases, according to Phillips?

Excerpted from "Dispelling Vaccination Myths," by Alan Phillips (cited April 1998). The complete, unedited text can be found at http://www.unc.edu/~aphillip/www/vaccine/informed.htm or by doing a search for "Dispelling Vaccination Myths." Reprinted by permission.

When my son began his routine vaccination series at age 2 months, I did not know there were any risks associated with immunizations. But the clinic's literature contained a contradiction: the chances of a serious adverse reaction to the DPT vaccine were 1 in 1750, while his chances of dying from pertussis each year were 1 in several million. When I pointed this out to the physician, he angrily disagreed, and stormed out of the room mumbling, "I guess I should read that sometime . . ." Soon thereafter I learned of a child who had been permanently disabled by a vaccine, so I decided to investigate for myself. My findings have so alarmed me that I feel compelled to share them; hence, this report.

Health authorities credit vaccines for disease declines, and assure us of their safety and effectiveness. Yet these seemingly rock-solid assumptions are directly contradicted by government statistics, medical studies, Food and Drug Administration (FDA) and Centers for Disease Control (CDC) reports, and reputable research scientists from around the world. In fact, infectious diseases declined steadily for decades prior to vaccinations, U.S. doctors report thousands of serious vaccine reactions each year including hundreds of deaths and permanent disabilities, fully vaccinated populations have experienced epidemics, and researchers attribute dozens of chronic immunological and neurological conditions to mass immunization programs.

There are hundreds of published medical studies documenting vaccine failure and adverse effects, and dozens of books written by doctors, researchers, and independent investigators that reveal serious flaws in immunization theory and practice. Ironically, most pediatricians and parents are completely unaware of these findings. However, this has begun to change in recent years, as a growing number of parents and healthcare providers around the world are becoming aware of the problems and starting to question the use of widespread, mandatory vaccinations.

My point is not to tell anyone whether or not to vaccinate, but rather, with the utmost urgency, to point out some very good reasons why everyone should examine the facts before deciding whether or not to submit to the procedure. As a new parent, I was shocked to discover the absence of a legal mandate or professional ethic requiring pediatricians to be fully informed, and to see first-hand the prevalence of physicians who are applying practices based on incomplete—and in some cases, outright mis—information.

Though only a brief introduction, this report contains sufficient evidence to warrant further investigation by all concerned, which I highly recommend. You will find that this is the only way to get an objective view, as the controversy is a highly emotional one.

A note of caution: Be careful trying to discuss this subject with a pediatrician. Most have staked their identities and reputations on the presumed safety and effectiveness of vaccines, and thus have difficulty acknowledging evidence to the contrary. The first pediatrician I attempted to share my findings with yelled angrily at me when I calmly brought up the subject. The misconceptions have very deep roots.

VACCINATION MYTH #1:

"Vaccines are completely safe . . ."

. . . *or are they?*

The FDA's VAERS (Vaccine Adverse Effects Reporting System) receives about 11,000 reports of serious adverse reactions to vaccination annually, some 1% (112+) of which are deaths from vaccine reactions. The majority of these reports are made by doctors, and the majority of deaths are attributed to the pertussis (whooping cough) vaccine, the "P" in DPT. This figure alone is alarming, yet it is only the "tip of the iceberg." The FDA estimates that only about 10% of adverse reactions are reported, a figure supported by two National Vaccine Information Center (NVIC) investigations. In fact, the NVIC reported that "In New York, only one out of 40 doctor's offices [2.5%] confirmed that they report a death or injury following vaccination"—97.5% of vaccine-related deaths and disabilities go unreported there. Implications about the integrity of medical professionals aside (doctors are *legally required* to report serious adverse events), these findings suggest that vaccine deaths actually occurring each year may be well over 1,000.

With pertussis, the number of vaccine-related deaths dwarfs the number of disease deaths, which have been about 10 annually for recent years according to the CDC, and only 8 in 1993, the last peak-incidence year (pertussis runs in 3–4 year cycles, though vaccination certainly doesn't). Simply put, the vaccine is 100 times more deadly than the disease. Given the many instances in which highly vaccinated populations have contracted disease (see Myth #2), and the fact that the vast majority of disease decline this century occurred before compulsory vaccinations (pertussis deaths declined 79% prior to vaccines; see Myth #3), this comparison is a valid one—and this enormous number of vaccine casualties can hardly be considered a necessary sacrifice for the benefit of a disease-free society.

Unfortunately, the vaccine-related-deaths story doesn't end here. Both national and international studies have shown vaccination to be a cause of SIDS (SIDS is "Sudden Infant Death Syndrome," a "catch-all" diagnosis given when the specific cause of death is unknown; estimates range from 5,000–10,000 cases each year in the U.S.). One study found the peak incidence of SIDS occurred at the ages of 2 and 4 months in the U.S., precisely when the first two routine immunizations are given, while another found a clear pattern of correlation extending three weeks after immunization. Another study found that 3,000 children die within 4 days of vaccination each year in the U.S. (amazingly, the authors reported no SIDS/vaccine relationship), while yet another researcher's studies led to the conclusion that half of SIDS cases—that would be 2,500 to 5,000 infant deaths in the U.S. each year—are caused by vaccines.

LONG-TERM EFFECTS OF VACCINES

Few serious attempts have been made to discover the long-term effects of injecting foreign proteins and toxic substances into the healthy bodies of innocent infants. In fact, research focusing on possible correlations between vaccines and autoimmune diseases and neurologically-based disorders (i.e., multiple sclerosis, cerebral palsy, Guillain-Barre syndrome, cancer, AIDS) is just beginning. For example, one medical researcher, Dr. Richard Moskowitz, recently concluded that the unnatural process of vaccination can lead to slow viruses developing in the body. These may bring about the "far less curable chronic diseases of the present."

Neil Miller, *Vaccines: Are They Really Safe and Effective?* 1996.

There are studies that claimed to find no SIDS-vaccine relationship. However, many of these were invalidated by yet another study which found that "confounding" had skewed their results in favor of the vaccine. Shouldn't we err on the side of caution? Shouldn't any credible correlation between vaccines and infant deaths be just cause for meticulous, widespread monitoring of the vaccination status of all SIDS cases? In the mid 70's Japan raised their vaccination age from 2 months to 2 years; their incidence of SIDS dropped dramatically. In spite of this, the U.S. medical community has chosen a posture of denial. Coroners refuse to check the vaccination status of SIDS victims, and unsuspecting families continue to pay the price, unaware of the dangers and denied the right to make a choice. . . .

Vaccinations cost us much more than just the lives and health of our children. The U.S. Federal Government's National Vaccine Injury Compensation Program (NVICP) has paid out over $724.4 million to parents of vaccine injured and killed children, in taxpayer dollars. The NVICP has received over 5,000 petitions since 1988, including over 700 for vaccine-related deaths, and there are still over 2,800 total death and injury cases pending that may take years to resolve. Meanwhile, pharmaceutical companies have a captive market: vaccines are legally mandated in all 50 U.S. states (though legally avoidable in most . . .), yet these same companies are "immune" from accountability for the consequences of their products. Furthermore, they have been allowed to use "gag orders" as a leverage tool in vaccine damage legal settlements to prevent disclosure of information to the public about vaccination dangers. Such arrangements are clearly unethical; they force a nonconsenting American public to pay for vaccine manufacturer's liabilities, while attempting to ensure that this same public will remain ignorant of the dangers of their products.

It is interesting to note that insurance companies (who do the best liability studies) refuse to cover vaccine adverse reactions. Profits appear to dictate both the pharmaceutical and insurance companies' positions.

Vaccination Truth #1: "Vaccination causes significant death and disability at an astounding personal and financial cost to families and taxpayers."

VACCINATION MYTH #2:
"Vaccines are very effective . . ."
  . . . or are they?
The medical literature has a surprising number of studies documenting vaccine failure. Measles, mumps, smallpox, polio and Hib outbreaks have all occurred in vaccinated populations. In 1989 the CDC reported: "Among school-aged children, [measles] outbreaks have occurred in schools with vaccination levels of greater than 98 percent. [They] have occurred in all parts of the country, including areas that had not reported measles for years." The CDC even reported a measles outbreak in a documented 100 percent vaccinated population. A Mayo Clinic Vaccine Research Group study examining this phenomenon concluded, *"The apparent paradox is that as measles immunization rates rise to high levels in a population, measles becomes a disease of immunized persons."* A 1996 study published in *Clinical Immunology and Immunopathology* found that measles vaccination *"produces immune suppression which contributes to an increased susceptibility to other infections."* These studies suggests that the goal of complete immunization is actually

counterproductive, a notion underscored by instances in which epidemics followed complete immunization of entire countries. Japan experienced yearly increases in smallpox following the introduction of compulsory vaccines in 1872. By 1892, there were 29,979 deaths, and all had been vaccinated. Early in this century, the Philippines experienced their worst smallpox epidemic ever after 8 million people received 24.5 million vaccine doses; the death rate quadrupled as a result. In 1989, the country of Oman experienced a widespread polio outbreak six months after achieving complete vaccination. In the U.S. in 1986, writes Neil Miller, 90% of 1,300 pertussis cases in Kansas were "*adequately vaccinated.*" 72% of pertussis cases in the 1993 Chicago outbreak were fully up to date with their vaccinations.

Vaccination Truth #2: "Evidence suggests that vaccination is an unreliable means of preventing disease."

VACCINATION MYTH #3:

"Vaccines are the main reason for low disease rates in the U.S. today . . ."

. . . or are they?

According to the British Association for the Advancement of Science, childhood diseases decreased 90% between 1850 and 1940, paralleling improved sanitation and hygiene practices, well before mandatory vaccination programs. Infectious disease deaths in the U.S. and England declined steadily by an average of about 80% during the twentieth century (measles mortality declined over 97%) prior to vaccinations. In Great Britain, the polio epidemics peaked in 1950, and had declined 82% by the time the vaccine was introduced there in 1956. Thus, at best, vaccinations can be credited with only a small percentage of the overall decline in disease related deaths this century. Yet even this small portion is questionable, as the rate of decline remained virtually the same after vaccines were introduced. Furthermore, European countries that refused immunization for smallpox and polio saw the epidemics end along with those countries that mandated it. (In fact, both smallpox and polio immunization campaigns were followed initially by significant disease incidence *increases*; during smallpox vaccination campaigns, other infectious diseases continued their declines in the absence of vaccines. In England and Wales, smallpox disease and vaccination rates eventually declined simultaneously over a period of several decades.) It is thus impossible to say whether or not vaccinations contributed to the continuing decline in disease death rates, or if the same forces which brought about the initial declines—improved sanitation, hygiene, improvements in diet, natural disease cycles—were simply unaffected by the vaccination programs. Underscoring this conclusion was a World Health Organization report which found that the disease and mortality rates in third world countries have no direct correlation with immunization procedures or medical treatment, but are closely related to the standard of hygiene and diet. Credit given to vaccinations for our current disease incidence has simply been grossly exaggerated, if not outright misplaced.

Vaccine advocates point to incidence statistics rather than mortality as proof of vaccine effectiveness. However, statisticians tell us that mortality statistics can be a better measure of incidence than the incidence figures themselves, for the simple reason that the quality of reporting and record-keeping is much higher on fatalities. For instance, a recent survey in New York City revealed that only 3.2% of pediatricians were actually reporting measles cases to the health department. In 1974, the CDC determined that there were 36 cases of measles in Georgia, while the Georgia State Surveillance System reported 660 cases. In 1982, Maryland state health officials blamed a pertussis epidemic on a television program, "D.P.T.—Vaccine Roulette," which warned of the dangers of DPT; however, when former top virologist for the U.S. Division of Biological Standards, Dr. J. Anthony Morris, analyzed the 41 cases, only 5 were confirmed, and all had been vaccinated. Such instances as these demonstrate the fallacy of incidence figures, yet vaccine advocates tend to rely on them indiscriminately.

Vaccination Truth #3: "It is unclear what impact vaccines had on the infectious disease declines that occurred throughout this century."

VACCINATION MYTH #4:

"Vaccination is based on sound immunization theory and practice . . ."

. . . *or is it?*

The clinical evidence for vaccinations is their ability to stimulate antibody production in the recipient, a fact which is not disputed. What is not clear, however, is whether or not such antibody production constitutes immunity. For example, agamma globulin-anemic children are incapable of producing antibodies, yet they recover from infectious diseases almost as quickly as other children. Furthermore, a study published by the British Medical Council in 1950 during a diphtheria epidemic concluded that there was no relationship between antibody count and disease incidence; researchers found resistant people with extremely low antibody counts and sick people with high counts. Natural immunization is a complex phenomenon involving many organs and systems; it cannot be fully replicated by the artificial stimulation of antibody production.

Research also indicates that vaccination commits immune cells to the specific antigens involved in the vaccine, rendering them incapable of reacting to other infections. Our immunological reserve may thus actually be reduced, causing a generally lowered resistance.

Another component of immunization theory is "herd immunity," which states that when enough people in a community are immunized, all are protected. As Myth #2 revealed, there are many documented instances showing just the opposite—fully vaccinated populations do contract diseases; with measles, this actually seems to be the direct result of high vaccination rates. A Minnesota state epidemiologist concluded that the Hib vaccine increases the risk of illness when a study revealed that vaccinated children were five times more likely to contract meningitis than unvaccinated children.

Carefully selected epidemiological studies are yet another justification for vaccination programs. However, many of these may not be legitimate sources from which to draw conclusions about vaccine effectiveness. For example, if 100 people are vaccinated and 5 contract the disease, the vaccine is declared to be 95% effective. But if only 10 of the 100 were actually exposed to the disease, then the vaccine was really only 50% effective. Since no one is willing to directly expose an entire population to disease—even a fully vaccinated one—vaccine effectiveness rates may not indicate a vaccine's true effectiveness.

Yet another surprising concern about immunization practice is its assumption that all children, regardless of age, are virtually the same. An 8 pound 2-month-old receives the same dosage as a 40 pound 5-year-old. Infants with immature, undeveloped immune systems may receive five or more times the dosage (relative to body weight) as older children. Furthermore, the number of "units" within doses has been found upon random testing to range from ½ to 3 times what the label indicates; manufacturing quality controls appear to tolerate a rather large margin of error. "Hot Lots"—vaccine lots with disproportionately high death and disability rates—have been identified repeatedly by the NVIC, but the FDA refuses to intervene to prevent further unnecessary injury and deaths. In fact, they have never recalled a vaccine lot due to adverse reactions. Some would call this infanticide. . . .

Vaccination Truth #4: "Many of the assumptions upon which immunization theory and practice are based have been proven false in their application."

VACCINATION MYTH #5:

"Childhood diseases are extremely dangerous . . ."
   . . . or are they, really?

Most childhood infectious diseases have few serious consequences in today's modern world. Even conservative CDC statistics for pertussis during 1992–94 indicate a 99.8% recovery rate. In fact, when hundreds of pertussis cases occurred in Ohio and Chicago in the fall 1993 outbreak, an infectious disease expert from Cincinnati Children's Hospital said, *"The disease was very mild, no one died, and no one went to the intensive care unit."*

The vast majority of the time, childhood infectious diseases are benign and self-limiting. They may also impart lifelong immunity, whereas vaccine-induced immunity is only temporary. In fact, the temporary nature of vaccine immunity can create a more dangerous situation in a child's future. For example, the new chicken pox vaccine has an effectiveness estimated at 6–10 years. If effective, it will postpone the child's vulnerability until adulthood, when death from the disease is 20 times more likely. . . .

Not only are most infectious diseases rarely dangerous, but they can actually play a vital role in the development of a strong, healthy immune system. Persons who have not had measles have a higher incidence of certain skin diseases, degenerative diseases of bone and cartilage, and certain tumors, while absence of mumps has been linked to higher risks of ovarian cancer.

Vaccination Truth #5: "Dangers of childhood diseases are greatly exaggerated in order to scare parents into compliance with a questionable but profitable procedure."* . . .

SUMMARY

In the December 1994 *Medical Post*, Canadian author of the bestseller *Medical Mafia*, Guylaine Lanctot, M.D. stated, *"The medical authorities keep lying. Vaccination has been a disaster on the immune system. It actually causes a lot of illnesses. We are actually changing our genetic code through vaccination . . . 10 years from now we will know that the biggest crime against humanity was vaccines."* After an extensive study of the medical literature on vaccination, Dr. Viera Scheibner concluded that *"there is no evidence whatsoever of the ability of vaccines to prevent any diseases. To the contrary, there is a great wealth of evidence that they cause serious side effects."* John B. Classen, M.D., M.B.A. has stated, *"My data proves that the studies used to support immunization are so flawed that it is impossible to say if immunization provides a net benefit to anyone or to society in general. This ques-*

tion can only be determined by proper studies which have never been performed. The flaw of previous studies is that there was no long term follow up and chronic toxicity was not looked at. The American Society of Microbiology has promoted my research . . . and thus acknowledges the need for proper studies." To some these may seem like radical positions, but they are not unfounded. The continued denial of the evidence against vaccines only perpetuates the "Myths" and their negative consequences on our children and society. Aggressive and comprehensive scientific investigation is clearly warranted, yet immunization programs continue to expand in the absence of such research. Manufacturer profits are guaranteed, while accountability for the negative effects is conspicuously absent. This is especially sad given the readily available safe and effective alternatives.

Meanwhile, the race is on. According to the NVIC, there are over 250 new vaccines being developed for everything from earaches to birth control to diarrhea, with about 100 of these already in clinical trials. Researchers are working on vaccine delivery through nasal sprays, mosquitoes (yes, mosquitoes), and the fruits of "transgenic" plants in which vaccine viruses are grown. With every child (and adult, for that matter) on the planet a potential required recipient of multiple doses, and every healthcare system and government a potential buyer, it is little wonder that countless millions of dollars are spent nurturing the growing multi-billion dollar vaccine industry. Without public outcry, we will see more and more new vaccines required of us and our children. And while profits are readily calculable, the real human costs are being ignored.

Whatever your personal vaccination decision, make it an informed one; you have that right and responsibility. It is a difficult issue, but there is more than enough at stake to justify whatever time and energy it takes.

Do not use this report alone to make your vaccination decision: FIND OUT FOR YOURSELF!

| "To have a medical intervention as effective as vaccination in preventing disease and not use it would be unconscionable."

VACCINES ARE SAFE AND EFFECTIVE

Centers for Disease Control and Prevention

The Centers for Disease Control and Prevention (CDC) is a federal government agency that is charged with tracking disease and assisting state public health agencies. Its National Immunization Program (NIP) provides training, consultation, and technical services to state and local health departments in implementing immunization programs and in monitoring the safety of vaccines. The following viewpoint is taken from a CDC publication written for doctors and other health professionals to help them respond to parents' concerns about the safety and effectiveness of child vaccines. The CDC contends that vaccines are carefully monitored for safety and that failing to vaccinate a child increases his or her risk of injury or death due to disease.

As you read, consider the following questions:

1. How has the effectiveness of vaccines been demonstrated, according to the CDC?
2. According to the CDC, what steps does the Food and Drug Administration take to ensure vaccines are safe?
3. What two reasons does the CDC give for continued vaccination despite the low levels of disease in the United States?

Excerpted from "Six Common Misconceptions About Vaccination and How to Respond to Them," by the Centers for Disease Control and Prevention, at http://www.cdc.gov/nip/6mishom2.htm (March 1998).

As a practitioner giving vaccinations, you will encounter patients who have reservations about getting vaccinations for themselves or their children. There can be many reasons for fear of or opposition to vaccination. Some people have religious or philosophic objections. Some see mandatory vaccination as interference by the government into what they believe should be a personal choice. Others are concerned about the safety or efficacy of vaccines, or may believe that vaccine-preventable diseases do not pose a serious health risk. . . .

The purpose of this viewpoint is to address six common misconceptions about vaccination that are often cited by concerned parents as reasons to question the wisdom of vaccinating their children. If we can respond with accurate rebuttals perhaps we can not only ease their minds on these specific issues but discourage them from accepting other anti-vaccine "facts" at face value. Our goal is not to browbeat parents into vaccinating, but to make sure they have accurate information with which to make an informed decision.

1. Diseases had already begun to disappear before vaccines were introduced, because of better hygiene and sanitation.

Statements like this are very common in anti-vaccine literature, the intent apparently being to suggest that vaccines are not needed. Improved socioeconomic conditions have undoubtedly had an indirect impact on disease. Better nutrition, not to mention the development of antibiotics and other treatments, have increased survival rates among the sick; less crowded living conditions have reduced disease transmission; and lower birth rates have decreased the number of susceptible household contacts. But looking at the actual incidence of disease over the years can leave little doubt of the significant *direct* impact vaccines have had, even in modern times. For example, . . . a graph showing the reported incidence of measles from 1920 to the present . . . [would show] periodic peaks and valleys throughout the years, but the real, permanent drop coincided with the licensure and wide use of measles vaccine beginning in 1963. Graphs for other vaccine-preventable diseases show a roughly similar pattern, showing a significant drop in cases corresponding with the advent of vaccine use. Are we expected to believe that better sanitation caused incidence of each disease to drop, just at the time a vaccine for that disease was introduced?

OTHER EXAMPLES OF DISEASE REDUCTION

Hib vaccine is another good example, because Hib disease was prevalent until just a few years ago, when conjugate vaccines that can be used for infants were finally developed. (The polysaccharide vaccine previously available could not be used for infants, in whom most of cases of the disease were occurring.) Since sanitation is not better now than it was in 1990, it is hard to attribute the virtual disappearance of Hib disease in children in recent years (from an estimated 20,000 cases a year to 1,419 cases in 1993, and dropping) to anything other than the vaccine.

Varicella [chicken pox] can also be used to illustrate the point, since modern sanitation has obviously not prevented nearly 4 million cases each year in the United States. If diseases were disappearing, we should expect varicella to be disappearing along with the rest of them. But nearly all children in the United States get the disease today, just as they did 20 years ago or 80 years ago. Based on experience with the varicella vaccine in studies before licensure, we can expect the incidence of varicella to drop significantly now that a vaccine has been licensed for the United States.

Finally, we can look at the experiences of several developed countries after they let their immunization levels drop. Three countries—Great Britain, Sweden, and Japan—cut back the use of pertussis vaccine because of fear about the vaccine. The effect was dramatic and immediate. In Great Britain, a drop in pertussis vaccination in 1974 was followed by an epidemic of more than 100,000 cases of pertussis and 36 deaths by 1978. In Japan, around the same time, a drop in vaccination rates from 70% to 20%–40% led to a jump in pertussis from 393 cases and no deaths in 1974 to 13,000 cases and 41 deaths in 1979. In Sweden, the annual incidence rate of pertussis per 100,000 children 0–6 years of age increased from 700 cases in 1981 to 3,200 in 1985. It seems clear from these experiences that not only would diseases not be disappearing without vaccines, but if we were to stop vaccinating, they would come back. . . .

2. *The majority of people who get disease have been vaccinated.*

This is another argument frequently found in anti-vaccine literature—the implication being that this proves vaccines are not effective. In fact it is true that in an outbreak those who have been vaccinated often outnumber those who have not—even with vaccines such as measles, which we know to be about 98% effective when used as recommended.

AN APPARENT PARADOX

This apparent paradox is explained by two factors. First, no vaccine is 100% effective. To make vaccines safer than the disease, the bacteria or virus is killed or weakened (attenuated). For reasons related to the individual, not all vaccinated persons develop immunity. Most routine childhood vaccines are effective for 85% to 95% of recipients. Second, in a country such as the United States the people who have been vaccinated vastly outnumber those who have not. How these two factors work together to result in outbreaks in which the majority of cases have been vaccinated can be more easily understood by looking at a hypothetical example:

In a high school of 1,000 students, none has ever had measles. All but 5 of the students have had two doses of measles vaccine, and so are fully immunized. The entire student body is exposed to measles, and every susceptible student becomes infected. The 5 unvaccinated students will be infected, of course. But of the 995 who *have* been vaccinated, we would expect several not to respond to the vaccine. The efficacy rate for two doses of measles vaccine can be as high as >99%. In this class, 7 students do not respond, and they, too, become infected. Therefore 7 of 12, or about 58%, of the cases occur in students who have been fully vaccinated.

As you can see, this doesn't prove the vaccine didn't work—only that most of the children in the class had been vaccinated,

---

RISK FROM DISEASE VS. RISK FROM VACCINES

Disease:

- *Measles*: Pneumonia: 1 in 20, Encephalitis: 1 in 2,000, Death: 1 in 3,000
- *Mumps*: Encephalitis: 1 in 300
- *Rubella*: Congenital Rubella Syndrome: 1 in 4 (if woman becomes infected early in pregnancy)

Vaccines:

- *MMR*: Encephalitis or severe allergic reaction: 1 in 1,000,000

Disease:

- *Diphtheria*: Death: 1 in 20
- *Tetanus*: Death: 3 in 100
- *Pertussis*: Pneumonia: 1 in 8, Encephalitis: 1 in 20, Death: 1 in 200

Vaccines:

- *DTP*: Continuous crying, then full recovery: 1 in 100, Convulsions or shock, then full recovery: 1 in 1,750, Acute encephalopathy: 0–10.5 in 1,000,000, Death: None proven

Centers for Disease Control and Prevention, *Six Common Misconceptions About Vaccination*, 1996.

so those who were vaccinated and did not respond outnumbered those who had not been vaccinated. Looking at it another way, 100% of the children who had not been vaccinated got measles, compared with less than 1% of those who had been vaccinated. Measles vaccine protected most of the class; if nobody in the class had been vaccinated, there would probably have been 1,000 cases of measles.

Vaccine "Hot Lots"

3. *There are "hot lots" of vaccine that have been associated with more adverse events and deaths than others. Parents should find the numbers of these lots and not allow their children to receive vaccines from them.*

This misconception got considerable publicity recently when vaccine safety was the subject of a television news program. First of all, the concept of a "hot lot" of vaccine as it is used in this context is wrong. It is based on the presumption that the more reports to the Vaccine Adverse Effects Reporting System (VAERS) a vaccine lot is associated with, the more dangerous the vaccine in that lot; and that by consulting a list of the number of reports per lot, a parent can identify vaccine lots to avoid.

This is misleading for two reasons:

1. VAERS is a system for reporting events that are *temporally associated* with receipt of vaccine; VAERS reports should not be interpreted to imply causality. In other words, a VAERS report does not mean that the vaccine caused the event. Statistically, a certain number of serious illnesses, even deaths, can be expected to occur by chance alone among children recently vaccinated. Although vaccines are known to cause minor, temporary side effects such as soreness or fever, there is little, if any, evidence linking vaccination with permanent health problems or death. The point is that just because an adverse event has been reported to VAERS does not mean it was caused by a vaccine.

2. Vaccine lots are not the same. The sizes of vaccine lots might vary from several hundred thousand doses to several million, and some are in distribution much longer than others. Naturally a larger lot or one that is in distribution longer will be associated with more adverse events, simply by chance. Also, more coincidental deaths are associated with vaccines given in infancy than later in childhood, since the background death rates for children are highest during the first year of life. So knowing that lot A has been associated with x number of adverse events while lot B has been associated with y number would not necessarily say anything about the relative safety of the two lots, even if the vaccine *did* cause the events.

Reviewing published lists of "hot lots" will not help parents identify the best or worst vaccines for their children. If the number and type of VAERS reports for a particular vaccine lot suggested that it was associated with more serious adverse events or deaths than are expected by chance, the Food and Drug Administration (FDA) has the legal authority to immediately recall that lot. To date, no vaccine lot in the modern era has been found to be unsafe on the basis of VAERS reports.

THE SAFETY OF VACCINES

All vaccine manufacturing facilities and vaccine products are licensed by the FDA. In addition, every vaccine lot is safety-tested by the manufacturer. The results of these tests are reviewed by FDA, who may repeat some of these tests as an additional protective measure. FDA also inspects vaccine-manufacturing facilities regularly to ensure adherence to manufacturing procedures and product-testing regulations, and reviews the weekly VAERS reports for each lot searching for unusual patterns. FDA would recall a lot of vaccine at the first sign of problems. There is no benefit to either the FDA or the manufacturer in allowing unsafe vaccine to remain on the market. The American public would not tolerate vaccines if they did not have to conform to the most rigorous safety standards. The mere fact that a vaccine lot is still in distribution says that the FDA considers it safe.

4. *Vaccines cause many harmful side-effects, illnesses, and even death—not to mention possible long-term effects we don't even know about.*

Vaccines are actually very safe, despite implications to the contrary in many anti-vaccine publications (which sometimes contain the number of reports received by VAERS, and allow the reader to infer that all of them represent genuine vaccine side effects). Most vaccine adverse events are minor and temporary, such as a sore arm or mild fever. These can often be controlled by taking acetaminophen before or after vaccination. More serious adverse events occur rarely (on the order of one per thousands to one per millions of doses), and some are so rare that risk cannot be accurately assessed. As for vaccines causing death, again so few deaths can plausibly be attributed to vaccines that it is hard to assess the risk statistically. Of all deaths reported to VAERS between 1990 and 1992, only one is believed to be even possibly associated with a vaccine. Each death reported to VAERS is thoroughly examined to ensure that it is not related to a new vaccine-related problem, but little or no evidence suggests that vaccines have contributed to any of the reported deaths. The Institute of Medicine in its 1994 report states that the risk of death from vaccines is "extraordinarily low."

DTP Vaccine and SIDS

One myth that won't seem to go away is that DTP vaccine causes sudden infant death syndrome (SIDS). This belief came about because a moderate proportion of children who die of SIDS have recently been vaccinated with DTP; and on the surface, this seems to point toward a causal connection. But this logic is faulty; you might as well say that eating bread causes car crashes, since most drivers who crash their cars could probably be shown to have eaten bread within the past 24 hours.

If you consider that most SIDS deaths occur during the age range when 3 shots of DTP are given, you would expect DTP shots to precede a fair number of SIDS deaths simply by chance. In fact, when a number of well-controlled studies were conducted during the 1980's, the investigators found, nearly unanimously, that the number of SIDS deaths temporally associated with DTP vaccination was within the range expected to occur by chance. In other words, the SIDS deaths would have occurred even if no vaccinations had been given. In fact, in several of the studies children who had recently gotten a DTP shot were *less* likely to get SIDS. The Institute of Medicine reported that "all controlled studies that have compared immunized versus non-immunized children have found either no association . . . or a decreased risk . . . of SIDS among immunized children" and concluded that "the evidence does not indicate a causal relation between [DTP] vaccine and SIDS."

But looking at risk alone is not enough—you must always look at both risks and benefits. Even one serious adverse effect in a million doses of vaccine cannot be justified if there is no benefit from the vaccination. If there were no vaccines, there would be many more cases of disease, and along with them, more serious side effects and more deaths. For example, according to an analysis of the benefit and risk of DTP immunization, if we had no immunization program in the United States, pertussis cases could increase 71-fold and deaths due to pertussis could increase 4-fold. Comparing the risk from disease with the risk from the vaccines can give us an idea of the benefits we get from vaccinating our children. (see table)

The fact is that a child is far more likely to be seriously injured by one of these diseases than by any vaccine. While any serious injury or death caused by vaccines is too many, it is also clear that the benefits of vaccination greatly outweigh the slight risk, and that many, many more injuries and deaths would occur without vaccinations. In fact, to have a medical intervention as effective as vaccination in preventing disease and not use it would be unconscionable.

Research is underway by the U.S. Public Health Service to better understand which vaccine adverse events are truly caused by vaccines and how to reduce even further the already low risk of serious vaccine-related injury.

5. *Vaccine-preventable diseases have been virtually eliminated from the United States, so there is no need for my child to be vaccinated.*

It's true that vaccination has enabled us to reduce most vaccine-preventable diseases to very low levels in the United States. However, some of them are still quite prevalent—even epidemic—in other parts of the world. Travelers can unknowingly bring these diseases into the United States, and if we were not protected by vaccinations these diseases could quickly spread throughout the population, causing epidemics here. At the same time, the relatively few cases we currently have in the U.S. could very quickly become tens or hundreds of thousands of cases without the protection we get from vaccines.

TWO REASONS FOR CONTINUED VACCINATION

We should still be vaccinated, then, for two reasons. The first is to protect ourselves. Even if we think our chances of getting any of these diseases are small, the diseases still exist and can still infect anyone who is not protected. A few years ago in California a child who had just entered school caught diphtheria and died. He was the only unvaccinated pupil in his class.

The second reason to get vaccinated is to protect those around us. There is a small number of people who cannot be vaccinated (because of severe allergies to vaccine components, for example), and a small percentage of people don't respond to vaccines. These people are susceptible to disease, and their only hope of protection is that people around them are immune and cannot pass disease along to them. A successful vaccination program, like a successful society, depends on the cooperation of every individual to ensure the good of all. We would think it irresponsible of a driver to ignore all traffic regulations on the presumption that other drivers will watch out for him or her. In the same way we shouldn't rely on people around us to stop the spread of disease; we, too, must do what we can.

6. *Giving a child multiple vaccinations for different diseases at the same time increases the risk of harmful side effects and can overload the immune system.*

Children are exposed to many foreign antigens every day. Eating food introduces new bacteria into the body, and numerous bacteria live in the mouth and nose, exposing the immune system to still more antigens. An upper respiratory viral infection exposes a child to 4–10 antigens, and a case of "strep throat" to 25–50. According to *Adverse Events Associated with Childhood Vaccines*, a 1994 report from the Institute of Medicine, "In the face of these normal events, it seems unlikely that the number of separate antigens contained in childhood vaccines . . . would represent an appreciable added burden on the immune system that would be immunosuppressive." And, indeed, available scientific data show that simultaneous vaccination with multiple vaccines has no adverse effect on the normal childhood immune system.

A number of studies have been conducted to examine the effects of giving various combinations of vaccines simultaneously. In fact, neither the Advisory Committee on Immunization Practices (ACIP) nor the American Academy of Pediatrics (AAP) would recommend the simultaneous administration of any vaccines until such studies showed the combinations to be both safe and effective. These studies have shown that the recommended vaccines are as effective in combination as they are individually, and that such combinations carry no greater risk for adverse side effects. Consequently, both the ACIP and AAP recommend simultaneous administration of all routine childhood vaccines when appropriate. Research is under way to find ways to combine more antigens in a single vaccine injection (for example, MMR and chicken pox). This will provide all the advantages of the individual vaccines, but will require fewer shots.

PRACTICAL FACTORS

There are two practical factors in favor of giving a child several vaccinations during the same visit. First, we want to immunize children as early as possible to give them protection during the vulnerable early months of their lives. This generally means giving inactivated vaccines beginning at 2 months and live vaccines at 12 months. The various vaccine doses thus tend to fall due at the same time. Second, giving several vaccinations at the same time will mean fewer office visits for vaccinations, which saves parents both time and money and may be less traumatic for the child.

> "We . . . maintain that American
> citizens . . . should never be forced to
> engage in any medical procedure
> which carries the risk of injury or
> death against their will."

MANDATORY VACCINATION PROGRAMS VIOLATE PARENTS' INFORMED CONSENT RIGHTS

Barbara Loe Fisher

Barbara Loe Fisher is cofounder and president of the National Vaccine Information Center (NVIC), an organization formed in 1982 by parents whose children died or suffered injuries after being vaccinated (Fisher's oldest son suffered from multiple learning disabilities after an adverse reaction to a DPT vaccination in 1980 when he was two). The private association (originally called Dissatisfied Parents Together) works to help parents whose children have suffered adverse reactions to vaccines, monitors vaccine research and public policy, and opposes compulsory vaccination laws. In the following viewpoint, Fisher argues that government and health authorities have failed to be fully honest with parents about the risks of vaccines, which she contends have injured and killed many children. She asserts that no parents should be compelled to vaccinate their children.

As you read, consider the following questions:

1. What specific adverse reactions do some children have to vaccines, according to Fisher?
2. What information have doctors and vaccine manufacturers failed to communicate to parents, according to the author?

Adapted from Barbara Loe Fisher's opening statement to the Institute of Medicine Vaccine Safety Forum Workshop on Risk Communication and Vaccination, May 13, 1996 (full text available at http://www.halcyon.com/discovry/discovry/vaccine.html). Reprinted with the author's permission.

In 1988, Tina and her husband watched their healthy three-month-old son, Evan, get his first DPT shot and within hours react with a swollen leg, bouts of high pitched screaming, and a fever. In the following days he was unusually lethargic, then lost head control and, finally, suffered a seizure, collapsed and died. The coroner listed Evan's death as heart failure but the doctor told his parents that Evan was a victim of sudden infant death syndrome.

In 1994, Tina gave birth to a healthy baby girl. When nine-month-old Miranda got her second DPT and HIB vaccinations, within 48 hours she woke her parents up with a scream that ended in a loud shriek. Tina ran to her daughter's crib and found her in the middle of a seizure that was followed by a collapse. Tina gave her baby CPR to try to revive her but Miranda died at the hospital an hour later. This time the pathologists concluded, and the coroner agreed, the cause of death was a fatal reaction to DPT and HIB vaccines.

TRAGEDY IN THE FAMILY

In 1980, my fully vaccinated sister brought whooping cough into the family. Her three-year-old daughter had gotten 4 DPT shots but also got pertussis. Her three-week-old infant daughter, Sarah, was hospitalized with pertussis and had to be resuscitated many times. I will always remember listening to my sister describe her baby's terrifying struggle to breathe and how she was afraid her newborn daughter would die. Sarah recovered completely from her bout with whooping cough and is a healthy, bright 16-year-old today. But the baby with whooping cough in the hospital isolation room next to Sarah was not so lucky. She died.

In 1990, Lisa's first daughter was left with severe brain injuries after a reaction to DPT vaccine and was later awarded federal compensation for her injuries. When South Carolina health authorities found out that Lisa had not vaccinated her youngest daughter with pertussis vaccine, they started calling Lisa twice a week and showing up at her house unannounced, threatening to charge her with child abuse and take the child if she did not vaccinate. Lisa finally told them she had a gun and would leave the state to protect her child from vaccine damage if they did not leave her alone.

You cannot be in the presence of a profoundly vaccine damaged child and not know that child could be your own. And you cannot try to comfort a mother who has just buried a baby who has died from a vaccine or a disease and not know that you could be the one standing over the grave. When it happens to your child, the risks are 100 percent. . . .

WE WANT INFORMATION

Those of us who co-founded Dissatisfied Parents Together in 1982 and then opened the National Vaccine Information Center in 1989 shared one goal: the prevention of vaccine injuries and deaths through public education. At the core of our public education effort is the deeply held conviction that all American consumers, but particularly parents, should have access to more complete information about the risks of vaccines and diseases. Our children suffered because we were not informed parents.

During the course of our research into more than 50 years of medical literature, we discovered that scientists and doctors had discussed among themselves for decades how vaccines can cause injury and death both in lab animals and in humans. Vaccine manufacturers, providers and policymakers knew that vaccines were being created out of viruses and bacteria grown in potentially contaminated human and animal tissue cultures and that substances such as mercury derivatives and sodium chloride and aluminum were being added and that, although heat and formaldehyde and other chemicals were being used to theoretically detoxify or render the viruses and bacteria incapable of causing harm, there was no guarantee, only hope, that an unknown number of healthy vaccine recipients would not die or be injured. But they never bothered to tell the people who were being vaccinated.

This failure to communicate what medical science does and does not know about vaccine risks was, quite simply, perceived as a fundamental betrayal of trust by those who were being asked to take the risk.

AN EROSION OF TRUST

Then, after the National Childhood Vaccine Injury Act was passed in 1986, when the Departments of Health and Justice worked together to rewrite the law and withhold federal compensation from three quarters of all children with vaccine associated injuries applying for help; when contraindications were narrowed and sick children started being vaccinated in emergency rooms; when each new vaccine produced was recommended for mandatory use; and when government and industry subsequently joined together to launch a mass media campaign to achieve a 100 percent vaccination rate by denying vaccine risks exist or suggesting that, if risks do exist, they are only experienced by children who are genetically compromised, there was a further erosion of trust.

Despite scientific evidence documenting the ability of vaccines to cause injuries and death in more than 70 years of medical literature; in 35 years of civil lawsuits; in the court records of at least 1,000 individuals who have been able to obtain acknowledgement in the vaccine injury compensation program; and even despite evidence supplied by the Institute of Medicine in their published reports on vaccine adverse events in 1991 and 1994, U.S. government officials continue to promote the idea that children who die or are brain injured following vaccination have an underlying genetic disorder and that (a) either the vaccine simply triggered the inevitable; or (b) these children were predestined to die or become brain damaged even if no vaccine had ever been given. Without any empirical evidence whatsoever in most individual cases of vaccine associated death and brain damage, health officials repeat the seductive and dangerous mantra to pediatricians and parents alike when referring to children with vaccine associated health problems—underlying genetic disorder.

DECISIONS SHOULD NOT BE FORCED

Authorities argue that parents should vaccinate their children to protect society as a whole from epidemics. But if the vaccines offered true immunity only the unvaccinated would become ill. Therefore, decisions that affect your child's health should not be forced upon you by so-called experts who are not even willing (nor able) to take responsibility for their actions.

Neil Miller, *Vaccines: Are They Really Safe and Effective?*, 1996.

And so, when parents take the state mandated vaccine risk and it turns out that the risk for their child is 100 percent, everyone has been carefully pre-conditioned to accept the idea that the vaccine is not responsible. The doctor is not responsible. The vaccine manufacturer is not responsible. The government is not responsible. The genetically defective child is responsible.

How convenient. No need for questions to be asked. No need to report deaths and injuries following vaccination. No need to pull vaccine lots associated with high numbers of deaths and injuries off the market. No need to commit dollars or time to conduct scientific studies to find out exactly what vaccines do in the human body at the cellular and molecular biology level. No need to develop pathological profiles for vaccine injury and death or develop a genetic marker to separate out high risk children and save their lives. No need to be concerned about the immune and neurological dysfunction of these genetically defective individuals who have been legally required to sacrifice their lives on the battlefield of our nation's War on Disease.

And so the haunting question remains: just how many are being sacrificed? How many of the mentally retarded, epileptic, autistic, learning disabled, hyperactive, diabetic, asthmatic children in the inner cities and the suburbs and the big and small towns of America are part of that sacrifice?

QUESTIONING MANDATORY VACCINATION

With the repeal of the military draft in the 1970's, mandatory vaccination is the only law in America which requires a citizen, in effect, to risk his life for his country. And when the draft was in effect during times of war the difference was that the young men being required to risk their lives were 18 years old and had the right to choose to conscientiously object. They were not 8-hour- or 8-week-old infants incapable of making that decision for themselves.

More and more people are beginning to question the moral center of a law that allows a group of self-appointed medical, risk assessment and cost management experts within the State to decide that, in the name of disease control, it is acceptable to sacrifice the lives of certain individuals for the theoretical well being of the rest and then use Orwellian tactics to convince the public their decision is correct. Who should have the power to decide that chicken pox is as dangerous as smallpox and must be eradicated from the earth or that failure to get a second measles shot should be a reason to throw a boy in jail like 17-year-old Jacob was several weeks ago in Milwaukee? [*Author's Note: Sixteen-year-old Jacob Kallas was handcuffed, stripped, and jailed overnight because he hadn't shown public school or county health officials proof that he had gotten a second MMR (measles-mumps-rubella) shot. Jacob was stopped by police while driving his mother's van, which had expired license plates. When a routine police check found he was wanted on a juvenile warrant issued by the county (for failure to vaccinate), he was jailed before being released to his mother the next morning.*]

For many, this issue transcends mandatory vaccination and speaks to the heart of the individual liberties upon which our democracy was founded. Because if the State can tag, track down and force citizens against their will to risk injury and death with biologicals of unknown toxicity today, there will be no limit on what individual freedoms the State can take away in the name of the greater good tomorrow.

My son, for whom the risks of the whole cell pertussis vaccine were 100 percent, I have no doubt, was predisposed to reacting to vaccines because we have a family history of severe allergies to drugs, vaccines, foods and environmental antigens. My son, as a baby, was the most cognitively gifted of my three children. Genetically gifted, genetically predisposed.

How many of us will eventually die from what will one day be identified as a health disorder that is under genetic control? Probably most of us. And when medical science identifies genetic markers, shouldn't we have the right to decide whether or not to risk using products or taking actions which could injure us or hasten our deaths? Or will that power be given to an elite group of experts within the State who will decide who will live and who will die and when?

We Must Decide for Our Children

The only voice our children have until they are old enough to make life and death decisions for themselves is the voice that we, their parents, who know and love them best, give to them.

In the absence of scientific studies to compare all morbidity and mortality outcomes in vaccinated and unvaccinated individuals to determine scientific truth and with vaccine experts busy comforting themselves with the scientifically idiotic supposition that the risk of dying after eating bread is identical to the risk of dying after being injected with a vaccine containing toxins that are used to deliberately induce seizures and death in lab animals, more and more people are refusing to blindly trust and put their lives and the lives of their children in the hands of the experts. They are demanding the right to decide for themselves which risk to take and the right to select the kind of preventive health care that is appropriate for their family.

There are those who are attempting to paint the people calling for better science and the right to informed consent as antivaccine child abusers and traitors to their country. And all they are doing by falsely characterizing people who are only trying to be good parents and responsible citizens is to pave the way for the day when you will see Americans marching with their children in the streets; standing up in court and in front of the TV cameras; willing to go to jail to fight for their human and civil rights; and defending with their lives their moral obligation to obey the certain judgement of their conscience and protect their children from harm.

You cannot take away freedom and force people to violate their conscience and expect to get away with it. Maybe in the Gulag or in Peking. But not in America.

THE POSITION OF THE NATIONAL VACCINE INFORMATION CENTER

In this politically charged debate I believe there will be no winners, only losers, if the two sides fail to find a way to intelligently coexist. With that, I want to make it clear, hopefully for the last time, that the National Vaccine Information Center has never told anyone not to vaccinate. That is not a decision that is ours to make. We have always provided information on disease risks because we believe health care consumers should know how serious those risks can be. We do not advocate elimination of vaccines.

We maintain that the least toxic and most technologically advanced vaccines that can be produced should be made available to Americans as a preventive health care choice; that vaccine risks should be fully defined and communicated; and that high risk individuals should be identified.

Simultaneously, in the spirit of the Bill of Rights in the American constitution, the provisions of the Nuremberg Code and the Helsinki Declarations as well as the tenets embodied in the scriptures of every major religion, we also maintain that American citizens should have the right to informed consent; the freedom to obey the judgement of their conscience; and should never be forced to engage in any medical procedure which carries the risk of injury or death against their will.

"There's no evidence that current [vaccination] exemptions are causing major disease outbreaks. . . . But infectious diseases have a way of finding the chinks in a society's immunological armor."

OPPOSITION TO VACCINATION PROGRAMS IS MISGUIDED

Arthur Allen

In recent years a growing number of parents and medical establishment critics have raised concerns about the safety of vaccines and have expressed opposition to state regulations that make vaccinations a mandatory condition for school enrollment. In the following viewpoint, Arthur Allen charges that many anti-vaccination activists provide false or misleading information to the public and thereby discourage parents from vaccinating their children. By opposing universal vaccination and hampering efforts to increase immunization rates, he argues, vaccination critics may leave children at greater risk of becoming victims of disease outbreaks. Allen is a freelance journalist who frequently writes on scientific and medical matters

As you read, consider the following questions:

1. What is one major difference between the anti-vaccination critics of today and those of a century ago, according to Allen?
2. According to the author, how do the immunization rates of poor blacks compare with the U.S. average?
3. What has happened in other countries that have experienced vaccination declines, according to the author?

Reprinted from "Injection Rejection," by Arthur Allen, *The New Republic*, March 23, 1998, by permission of *The New Republic*. Copyright ©1998 by The New Republic, Inc.

President Bill Clinton's ongoing initiative to immunize every American child against infectious disease seems like the kind of safe-as-milk, baby-step health policy that everyone should love. The ultimate motherhood issue. But Clinton, presumably, didn't consult Len Horowitz. A former dentist-turned-"healthcare motivational speaker," Horowitz is carving out a new niche in the history of the paranoid style in American politics. His message: The AIDS and Ebola epidemics resulted from the contamination—possibly intentional—of common vaccines by the military-medico-industrial complex. The Rockefeller Foundation, the Centers for Disease Control (CDC), famed AIDS researcher Dr. Robert Gallo, and—yes—Henry Kissinger all figure in Horowitz's gallery of germ-warfare conspirators. Horowitz, who apparently honed his expertise on such matters by drilling teeth in Gloucester, Massachusetts, has urged the government to stop immunizing children until independent researchers can determine if the shots are spreading disease. He charges up to $3,500 to share his theories with holistic-medicine groups, survivalist conventions, and other pockets of suspiciousness. During the past couple of years, he has rarely lacked for speaking engagements.

THE NATION OF ISLAM

The pronouncements of Len Horowitz might safely be filed away next to the *Protocols of the Elders of Zion* and the Roswell alien snapshots were it not for the fact that they are reaching an audience that has few antibodies to quackery. Most distressing to the Centers for Disease Control and the Food and Drug Administration (FDA), and to public health experts more generally, Horowitz and Louis Farrakhan have found each other.

According to a Nation of Islam official, Farrakhan heard Horowitz in 1997 on a talk-radio program in Phoenix and invited him to dinner. A joint news release followed from Horowitz and Dr. Abdul Alim Muhammad, Farrakhan's "minister of health and human services," calling for a moratorium on the immunization of Nation of Islam children. . . . Alarmed that already underimmunized ghetto populations were about to get goaded into forgoing vaccinations altogether, the National Medical Association—a mainstream professional group for black physicians—hastily arranged for public health officials to meet with Muhammad. . . . Afterward, Muhammad agreed to shelve the moratorium, at least temporarily. . . .

It appears unlikely that the Nation of Islam will truly dispense with immunizations, but, as it happens, Horowitz and Muhammad are merely the most baroque figures in a widespread and growing anti-vaccination movement. Its adherents range from clueless paranoids to parents and physicians with more or less genuine concerns about the safety of vaccinations and more or less solid scientific evidence to back them up. The movement poses a counterweight to what is arguably among the most encouraging developments in medicine: a generation of new vaccines for everything from aids and dengue fever to common childhood ear and gut infections.

VACCINATION AND ITS CRITICS

For years, vaccination has been a basic tenet of public health and one of its unqualified successes. The elimination of polio and diphtheria along with the decline of such potential killers as measles, mumps, whooping cough, and rubella are well-documented triumphs. A less known and more recent success story is that of the HIB vaccine, which inoculates children against the Haemophilus influenza type B bacteria, the main cause of bacterial meningitis. In 1984, the year before HIB was introduced, the disease struck about 20,000 Americans, mostly children, killing about 1,000 and causing brain damage or permanent hearing loss in a few thousand others. In 1997, only 150 cases of bacterial meningitis were reported.

Notwithstanding its achievements, vaccination is a counterintuitive biological process. Dead or weakened forms of a fearsome microorganism are injected into a healthy person, provoking an immune response—and often a few symptoms of the disease in question. The immune system's antibodies in turn protect the inoculated person from future attack from the "wild" forms of the germ. Since Edward Jenner smeared his first patient with cowpox to shield him from the more dangerous smallpox germs in 1796, immunization has inspired anxiety. The turn-of-the-century American anti-vaccinationist movement spread across the country and set off riots in Milwaukee. The "state quackery" of "compulsory blood poisoning" is an "abomination against God and human nature itself, and every intelligent, conscientious person regards it accordingly," a physiology professor wrote in a 1902 edition of The Vaccination Inquirer, the mouthpiece of the anti-vaccination movement (which was funded by a mail-order patent medicine company in Battle Creek, Michigan).

For the early anti-vaccinationists, immunization was a crime against hygiene and a get-rich scheme for doctors. But they didn't see it, exactly, as a political issue. Today, in contrast, some of the loudest opponents draw their support and arguments from left-meets-right anti-governmentalism. Horowitz, for example, has appeared at survivalist conventions cheek-by-jowl with right-wing militiamen and as a guest on Gary Null's *Natural Living*, a holistic health program that airs several times a week on left-wing Pacifica radio stations in Washington and New York. . . .

RISKS AND BENEFITS OF VACCINATIONS

I think that immunizations facilitate a natural process, the meetings of germs or of antigenic parts of germs with the immune system. Now, this is something that goes on anyway, so you're just facilitating it. The risks of immunization are often relatively small, and the benefits are great in terms of life-long immunity. . . .

I also think that the debate about immunization would only be going on in a country where the people are mostly immunized. I think if people in this country lived with these diseases, which still exist in some undeveloped countries, you wouldn't hear so many people questioning immunization. I think these are bad diseases, most of them, and they're must worse if you get them at older ages, which is more likely to happen if immunization is stopped, or if it's reduced.

Andrew Weil, *Natural Health*, November/December 1997.

[Other Null] anti-vaccination guests have included Viera Scheibner, a shrill Australian who insists that vaccines suppress immunity. (Scheibner obfuscated so wildly during a speaking tour of Australia in 1997 that *The Skeptic* magazine honored her with its annual Bent Spoon Award for Australia's biggest charlatan.) One Null show that aired December 17, 1997, on WPFW in Washington featured a Brooklyn "researcher" named Curtis Cost, who shared the following pearls of wisdom: "If you take the measles vaccine, you have a sixty, sixty-five percent chance of getting measles. If you take polio vaccine, you have a roughly eighty, eighty-seven percent chance you will get polio."

This is, of course, pure rubbish. Nevertheless, if you follow the foolishness to its source, you find that there are some real problems with vaccines.

A VICTIM OF ITS OWN SUCCESS

In a sense, mass childhood immunization has become a victim of its own success. Infant mortality rates in the U.S. are a quarter of what they were in 1950. The average child's risk of contracting polio, measles, or diphtheria is vanishingly low. No one questioned whether Normandy had been worth it after Hitler was crushed. But, the more the killer germs of the century (with the exception of HIV) fade from memory, the more the public's attention focuses on the adverse reactions vaccines themselves inevitably, if only occasionally, cause.

Take the polio scourge. "Polio was such a frightening specter that a few people's bad reactions to the vaccine simply didn't register," says Dr. Edgar Marcuse, chair of the National Vaccine Advisory Committee. "But the diseases that terrified our grandparents are no longer part of anyone's experience." While "wild" polio struck 21,269 people in 1952, it has not been reported in the United States since 1979. Since then, however, oral polio vaccines have given about 200 people the crippling disease. While that's awful enough if one of the 200 happens to be your child, it's still just one in 2.4 million doses—pretty good odds by any measure.

THE NATIONAL VACCINE INFORMATION CENTER

Another illustrative case study is the controversy over the whole-cell pertussis vaccine—the P in the DPT shot. In 1982, a group of parents who were convinced that the vaccine had harmed their children began organizing to press the government to do something about it. Barbara Loe Fisher is the president of the group, the National Vaccine Information Center, which is run out of a second-story office in a strip mall in suburban Vienna, Virginia. Fisher's oldest child, now 20, suffered a seizure and became learning-disabled after his fourth DPT shot in 1979. "The afternoon after the shot I went up to his room, and he was sitting in his little chair, staring straight ahead," she says in an interview. "I held him, and he pitched forward, with his eyes rolling around in his head. Later that night he had terrible diarrhea and then he slept, and I couldn't wake him. He's never been the same."

To be sure, Fisher's group has had at least some salutary impact: its pressure helped spur development of the even safer acellular pertussis vaccine, which became widely available in 1997. And, in 1986, after thousands of lawsuits against vaccine manufacturers threatened the supply of cheap vaccines, Fisher's group, the vaccine industry, and the CDC pushed Congress to pass the National Childhood Vaccine Injury Act. That act created a no-fault claims court, funded by a levy on vaccines, where the parents of sickened or dead children could collect compensation.

The vaccine court has handed out cash to more than 2,600 people whose children died or were seriously injured after vaccination—with DPT, in a large majority of the cases. Yet, while that number must be read as a tacit admission that vaccines carry some risk, neither it nor the 63,000 vaccine reactions (including 1,094 deaths) recorded in the past seven years by an FDA–CDC vaccine injury reporting system are necessarily proof of widespread vaccine failures. As CDC officials explain it, the reactions the system records are rarely distinctive enough for doctors to be sure a particular vaccine caused them. Babies suffer terrible illnesses, and since babies are often vaccinated it is likely that illness will occur not long after some immunization or another. In a 1994 report on vaccine safety, the Institute of Medicine reported that "the vast majority of deaths reported . . . are temporally but not causally related to vaccination." A later report amended that finding to acknowledge that the whole-cell pertussis vaccine could lead to permanent brain damage, but the bottom line, as one institute official puts it, remains that "a lot of bad things happen to small children that we don't understand."

VACCINE ANXIETY

The problem, in any event, is not the cases for which the government implicitly accepts responsibility, but the thousands— even millions—more that advocates like Fisher claim go unrecorded. "Kids get shots, something happens to them, and nobody makes the connection," says Fisher. "Why can't we do a better job of admitting we've got a problem here? Why can't they do the science to figure out what's going on?" Her group has trumpeted some recent studies that suggest vaccination may trigger autoimmune problems, in which the body attacks itself, and may be responsible for the increased incidence of diseases like asthma and diabetes and, for that matter, Gulf war syndrome. "You have to ask whether we're simply trading childhood sickness for chronic diseases," Fisher says.

This is a fascinating thought—and a rather disturbing one, particularly since it's so easy to disseminate. Although few scientists share it, there have been enough widely disparate studies on vaccine safety over the years that anybody—well, anyone with computer access to MEDLINE—can document anything he or she wants to say on his or her personal website, with all the sites hyperlinking back and forth in a frenetic group grope. Vaccine anxiety is the perfect symptom of what British medical writer Paul Hodgkin describes as postmodern medicine. "Utterly unquestioned biological givens are disintegrating all around us: the stability of the climate, the immutability of species . . . the unchangeable genetic makeup of one's unborn children," Hodgkin wrote recently in the *British Medical Journal*. With certainties fading, it is easy for people who feel medically vulnerable to build seductive hints and fragments into a coherent, if warped, belief system. "Trust is fragile," says Regina Rabinovich, chief of clinical studies in microbiology at the National Institute for Allergy and Infectious Diseases, "and in science we're not very good at proving the negative."

A PUBLIC HEALTH INITIATIVE

In 1994, Heather Whitestone became the first Miss America with a disability. She went deaf at the age of only 18 months, the initial news reports said, after suffering an adverse reaction to a DPT shot. In fact, as Whitestone's pediatrician later confirmed, it was not DPT but a bout of bacterial meningitis—the disease now nearly eliminated by the HIB vaccine—that cost Whitestone her hearing. The Whitestone case helped spur public health officials to begin an initiative to improve vaccine-safety information. They chose to run the project under the auspices of the Infectious Disease Society of America rather than the federal CDC. "There's too much anti-government, anti-industry sentiment out there," says one physician involved in the effort.

One of the major concerns of the project is the relatively low vaccination rate among poor blacks. In 1996, the CDC's National Immunization Survey found only 63 and 65 percent compliance with a recommended vaccination regimen for children in majority-black Newark and Detroit, respectively, compared to the U.S. average of 79 percent and the high of 88 percent in the state of Connecticut. Since vaccinations can be had for free, the major reasons for these low rates are clearly social—family disorganization and high dropout rates on the one hand, suspicion of the government on the other.

MANDATORY VACCINATION LAWS

Meanwhile, Barbara Loe Fisher recently embarked on a new crusade to win parents the federally guaranteed right to enroll their children in school without vaccinations if they don't believe in them. "It is not in the best interest of the citizens of this free society, or of public health officials in positions of authority, to use the heel of the boot of the state to crush all dissent to mandatory vaccination laws," she said in a recent speech. Fisher may not be Horowitz, but her position on mandatory vaccination worries public health officials—for good reason.

About half of one percent of all parents in the United States currently take advantage of religious exemptions from immunization, permitted in all states except for Mississippi and West Virginia, or of variously defined philosophical exemptions, which are allowed in 17 states. While public health officials generally see families who exempt their children as free-riders enjoying "herd immunity" without participating in the risk, they're usually willing to grant exemptions to any family that whines insistently enough, if only because a crackdown could provoke a more serious backlash. But with Fisher and others stirring up more support, public health officials worry that the anti-vaccination movement will gain footholds in the socially isolated groups that have distorted views of reality—and are, already, at greater risk of disease. Farrakhan's dalliance with Horowitz, for example, enraged many black physicians because they fear the target population's reliance on urban legends. "It's one thing to talk about AIDS as genocide and a whole different thing to fan the flames of mistrust and fear about immunizations," says Stephen Thomas, director of the Institute for Minority Health Research at Emory University's school of public health. "We know [vaccines] save lives."

There's no evidence that current exemptions are causing major disease outbreaks in the United States—at least for now. But infectious diseases have a way of finding the chinks in a society's immunological armor. In the January 31, 1998, issue of The Lancet, epidemiologists led by Eugene Gangarosa of Emory University charted the return of whooping cough after a decline of DPT shots in countries that had vaccination scares during the late 1970s. In Japan, after the deaths of two children who had gotten DPT shots in 1974, the percentage of school-age children receiving the pertussis vaccine fell from 80 percent to ten percent. Whooping cough, which had nearly disappeared, returned with a vengeance: in 1979, there were 13,000 cases and 41 deaths. Similar outbreaks followed declining vaccine coverage in Australia, Britain, and Sweden. The most crushing evidence of the continued need for vaccines comes from Russia, where crumbling public health services and Rasputin-like anti-vaccinationists have led to a collapse of immunizations in many areas and an explosion of long-dormant infectious diseases. In 1995, to cite the most tragic statistic, 1,700 Russians died of diphtheria, a disease of the 1920s.

RISKING MORE OUTBREAKS

In the United States, officials have gotten some sense of the opportunism of infectious diseases by studying small outbreaks. Of the 508 measles cases reported in 1996, 107 occurred in and around the town of St. George, Utah. In a fascinating study of that outbreak, CDC epidemiologists were able to demonstrate just how risky a few unvaccinated children could be. The St. George area has a high rate of schoolchildren with religious and philosophical exemptions from vaccination. Of the 107 measles cases, 48 were in exempted, unvaccinated children who played the key role in spreading the disease. Measles takes two weeks to incubate, so officials were able to track six successive generations of the outbreak. According to Daniel Salmon, a fellow at the CDC, two of the three children in the first generation were unvaccinated. The measles vaccine is thought to be 95 percent effective, which accounts for the 59 vaccinated children who contracted the disease. As the outbreak slowly spread through successive generations, exposing more and more children, the germs eventually found the small percentage of kids whose vaccinations had failed.

Whooping cough has increased slightly in the United States since Fisher's movement got underway. No one has linked the two, but, as it happens, no one is more aware of the risks than Fisher herself. After her son's episode with the DPT shot, Fisher decided not to vaccinate her two younger children. And, in a peculiarly bitter twist of fate, of the several thousand U.S. cases of pertussis in 1992, two were Fisher's children. "I watched as my five-year-old daughter's face turned white," she recalled in a recent speech. "Her lips turned blue, and her eyes bulged out of her head during a paroxysm of whooping cough that I thought would take her life."

PERIODICAL BIBLIOGRAPHY

The following articles have been selected to supplement the diverse views presented in this chapter. Addresses are provided for periodicals not indexed in the *Readers' Guide to Periodical Literature*, the *Alternative Press Index*, the *Social Sciences Index*, or the *Index to Legal Periodicals and Books*.

David Bardell	"Nestling Cuckoos to Vaccination: A Commemoration of Edward Jenner," *BioScience*, December 1996.
Susan Brink	"Global Epidemics, Close to Home," *U.S. News & World Report*, October 28, 1996.
Mark Caldwell	"The Dream Vaccine," *Discover*, September 1997.
Alexander Cockburn	"All Things That Fall," *Nation*, October 14, 1996.
Alan W. Dove and Vincent R. Racaniello	"The Polio Eradication Effort: Should Vaccine Eradication Be Next?" *Science*, August 8, 1997.
Economist	"Rash Worries: How to Assess Scary Stories About Vaccines," April 11, 1998.
Michael Gianturco	"SmithKline's Promising Vaccines," *Forbes*, December 15, 1997.
Stephen S. Hall	"Vaccinating Against Cancer," *Atlantic Monthly*, April 1997.
Robert Pollock	"Shots in the Dark," *Reason*, November 1994.
Andrea Rock	"The Lethal Dangers of the Billion-Dollar Vaccine Business," *Money*, December 1996.
John Salamone	"A Father's Crusade," *Good Housekeeping*, January 1997.
Lisa Schlein	"Hunting Down the Last of the Poliovirus," *Science*, January 9, 1998.
Nathan Seppa	"The Dark Side of Immunizations?" *Science News*, November 22, 1997.
Evelyn Strauss	"Squirts for Squirts: Flu Guards Kids," *Science News*, July 19, 1997.
Andrew Weil and Richard Moskowitz	"The Vaccination Debate: Modern Miracle or Time Bomb?" *Natural Health*, November/December 1997. Available from 17 Station St., Brookline, MA 02146.
Catherine Winters	"Vaccine Tracker," *Parents*, November 1997.
Yun Lee Wolfe and Rick Chillo	"Don't Play Chicken," *Prevention*, September 1997.

HOW CAN FOOD-BORNE ILLNESSES BE PREVENTED?

CHAPTER PREFACE

In 1993 hundreds of children on the Pacific coast became sick after eating undercooked hamburgers served by Jack In The Box restaurants. The meat was found to be contaminated with a dangerous form of E. coli bacteria. Four children ultimately died. The company that owned the fast-food chain revamped its safety operations and eventually paid millions of dollars to settle legal claims brought by families of the victims. California, following the lead of other states, passed a law establishing minimum cooking temperatures for preparing hamburgers.

Unfortunately, the Jack In The Box case was not an isolated incident. Every week almost two hundred people in the United States, most of them children or elderly, die from diseases that were contracted from eating tainted food. The Centers for Disease Control and Prevention (CDC) has estimated that between 6 million and 33 million people each year come down with some form of food-borne illness. Meat is not the only food to be contaminated; E.coli and other microbes have been found in fruit juices and on lettuce and alfalfa sprouts. Disease-causing parasites have been found on imported raspberries and other fruit.

People disagree about whether the government should play a greater role in attempting to prevent food-borne diseases. Some have advocated greater government powers to monitor food. "Amid the national fervor for less government," stated Secretary of Agriculture Dan Glickman in calling for greater regulatory powers for his department, "it is the nearly unanimous sentiment of the American people that government should do more to ensure food safety." But others argue that it is unrealistic to expect the federal government, even with increased powers, to guarantee food safety. Michael T. Osterholm, Minnesota's head epidemiologist, argues that government inspection and testing cannot ensure the detection of all contaminated food because of the sheer volume of food that is produced: "It's like sticking your hand in one part of the haystack and saying the whole stack is free of needles."

Whether the government, food processors, food retailers, or individual consumers bear the primary responsibility for preventing food-borne illnesses is one of the underlying questions in the food safety debate. The following viewpoints discuss several proposals for preventing any repetition of the Jack In The Box incident and similar tragedies.

| "To attain the most food safety at a reasonable cost, it is important that consumers . . . accept some responsibility for their own actions in keeping food . . . safe."

CONSUMERS SHOULD PRACTICE SAFE FOOD-HANDLING HABITS TO PREVENT ILLNESSES

American Council on Science and Health

The American Council on Science and Health (ACSH) is an association of scientists and doctors who provide the public with information on scientific and public health issues. In the following viewpoint, the association describes food hazards posed by disease-producing agents such as bacteria and parasites. The ACSH argues that food-borne illness outbreaks are more effectively prevented through basic safety precautions on the part of consumers than through government inspection and regulation of food production and processing enterprises. Consumers should recognize that 100 percent risk-free food is an impossible goal and that changes in the food system to reduce risk of illness may significantly raise the cost of food, the organization concludes.

As you read, consider the following questions:
1. What classifications of food-borne illnesses does the ACSH describe?
2. In what ways can food be contaminated by bacteria and other disease agents, according to the ACSH?
3. According to the ACSH, where are poor sanitation practices most common?

Reprinted, with permission, from *Eating Safely: Avoiding Foodborne Illness*, a publication of the American Council on Science and Health, 1995 Broadway, 2nd floor, New York, NY 10023-5860.

Foodborne disease occurs when a person eats food contaminated with one or more disease producing agents. These include bacteria, parasites, viruses, fungi and their products as well as toxic substances not of microbial origin. The most certain proof that contaminated food is the cause of illness is the detection of the disease agent in both the patient and the remains of the food eaten by the patient. Food may be implicated when two or more people become ill with similar symptoms at approximately the same time after having eaten the same food. Food may also be suspected if the illness is one that is often or usually foodborne.

Most foodborne illnesses are very mild. As a consequence, it is difficult to gauge the true incidence or the rate of change of incidence of foodborne illness in the U.S. Only a small proportion of actual cases are reported. . . .

TYPES OF ILLNESSES

Many diseases are transmitted by foods, some of which may have serious health consequences. Food poisonings (intoxications) and infections are the two most common types; these sometimes occur in large outbreaks.

Intoxications occur when a chemical or toxin causes the body to malfunction. For example, poisons are produced by algae that cause "red tides." Seafoods contaminated with these poisons are not safe for consumption. Some bacteria also produce harmful toxins that are not destroyed in the cooking process. For example, staphylococcal enterotoxin has been found in some canned mushrooms and in hard-cooked eggs. Certain metals can also cause intoxications if present in sufficient quantity. Viable bacteria need not be present if a toxin remains as the result of previous growth in food. Growth of the organism in the body need not occur for the organism to have an effect.

Infections occur when ingested food contains living microorganisms that begin to multiply in the body. Normally, our gastrointestinal tract harbors many microbes, most of which do no harm. However, certain pathogenic bacteria, viruses or parasites occasionally contained in food can cause illness by producing poisons in the body or by directly attacking the lining of the digestive tract or other organs. Infectious agents usually take several hours to days to overcome the body's defenses and build up to levels that cause disease. Thus, the illness can occur long after eating. These infections are rarely fatal—the body's defenses usually win out, but only after a good deal of discomfort.

Other foodborne illnesses affect only certain people. Illnesses result when sensitive individuals ingest normal amounts of perfectly wholesome food, but have an allergic or intolerant reaction to a specific food component. Such sensitivities often run in families and are genetically based. . . .

How Do Disease Agents Get into Foods?

Some poisonous substances occur naturally in foods; others (including some of the deadliest) are produced by microorganisms, such as the toxin produced by *Clostridium botulinum*. Infectious microbes are very often present while foods are still in the field, sea or on the farm. Others are introduced if the food is mishandled during processing, distribution or preparation. . . .

It is simply not possible to produce raw food materials that are absolutely risk-free for everyone. Many plants are poisonous. Some of these can be eaten safely only after proper processing (e.g. soybeans, cassava). Others that are not poisonous routinely contain microbes that, given the chance, can cause foodborne disease. Food animals on farms carry microbes that can cause human disease. Fish and other seafood may be poisonous at times or may harbor parasites, bacteria or viruses that can threaten human health.

Agents that can cause human disease are ubiquitous in both land and sea; agricultural land carries additional disease agents when fertilized with animal manure or human waste. Animals can be produced free of disease agents, but only under conditions that would cause food to be prohibitively expensive. *Essentially all raw foods carry the risk of causing human disease if not properly cooked or handled until they are eaten.*

Handling and the Human Factor

"Handling" includes anything that happens to food from harvesting until the food is eaten. Harvest or slaughter, processing, storage, distribution, retailing, final preparation and serving—all offer chances for contamination, the introduction of disease agents.

It is very difficult to slaughter and eviscerate animals without getting intestinal contents, which contain bacteria that are infectious for humans, onto the edible portion of the carcass.

It is important that surfaces and utensils that have been in contact with raw meat and poultry not be used in handling cooked meats or other foods that will not be cooked before they are eaten unless they have been suitably cleaned. Even the liquid that drips from raw meat or poultry can get onto other foods or food-contact surfaces, resulting in "cross-contamination."

People are another important source of food contamination. Infected people who handle food can introduce infectious microbes into or onto the product. Most infectious agents that travel from person to person via food are shed primarily in feces. Although most of the precautions called for in food handling (e.g. wear hair restraints, don't sneeze or cough on the food) are a part of basic hygiene, they have very little to do with prevention of foodborne disease. An important precaution to prevent contamination of food with infectious agents from humans is thorough hand-washing after toilet use—especially after defecation. This applies to anyone who handles food, but particularly to those who do final preparation and serving, because any microorganism introduced at that late stage is likely still to be alive and infectious when the food is eaten. Hands can also carry cross-contamination (say, from raw food to cooked food), so they should be washed often during food handling.

Other significant sources of food contamination include insects, rodents, birds and water that contains sewage. Facilities in which food is handled must be carefully monitored for these contamination sources.

TIME-TEMPERATURE RELATIONSHIPS

The length of time food has spent at various temperatures affects the safety of the final product. Canned, irradiated, or otherwise "shelf-stable" foods can be stored safely at room temperature for long periods. Other foods such as flour, sugar, honey, etc., have so little available moisture that microbes will not grow in them, regardless of storage temperature. However, many foods are "perishable"—microbes can grow in them and cause spoilage. Of course, low-moisture foods become perishable when water is added, and canned foods become perishable when the can is opened. Only a few of the bacteria and molds that cause spoilage are agents of human disease.

Perishable foods support the growth of disease agents, which is why the time spent at temperatures between 40° and 140°F (the "danger zone") must be minimized. Hot foods must be kept hot, and cold foods must be kept cold. Food that is heated and then stored cold must be chilled rapidly; this may require dividing a large quantity among small or shallow containers so that the heat is removed efficiently. Chilled food that is to be cooked or reheated should be heated rapidly and thoroughly.

While preventing spoilage is a concern, the principal reason to avoid "temperature abuse" is to prevent the multiplication of bacteria and, to a lesser extent, molds on food. At certain temperatures, bacteria can build up to highly infectious levels or produce poisons that threaten human health. Molds tend to grow more slowly, but may produce poisons. Parasites and viruses cannot multiply in foods, but can remain infectious. Poisons present in raw food can not increase at improper storage temperatures, but some can be reduced by heating. Other factors that influence the growth of disease and spoilage microbes are moisture, acidity, natural and artificial preservatives, nutrients, the presence or absence of oxygen and the presence of other bacteria competing for the same resources. . . .

HOW SAFE IS SAFE ENOUGH?

A no-risk national food supply is not an attainable goal. A small increase of safety to an already safe food supply would require large sums of money. This huge cost must be weighed against potential benefit. U.S. consumers now spend less time earning money for their food than do people in any other country. Still, in 1988 this inexpensive food supply was not always accessible to at least 20 million people in the U.S. who were undernourished according to the standards of the World Health Organization. This situation is unlikely to have improved since then, and may well have worsened. Any change that increases the cost of food, with or without good reason, will mean that more people go hungry. Therefore, the food safety agenda should only be modified after very careful consideration of the risks *versus* the benefits.

GOLDEN RULES FOR SAFE FOOD PREPARATION

1. Choose foods processed for safety.

2. Cook food thoroughly.

3. Eat cooked food immediately.

4. Store cooked foods carefully.

5. Reheat cooked foods thoroughly.

6. Avoid contact between raw and cooked foods.

7. Wash hands repeatedly.

8. Keep all kitchen surfaces meticulously clean.

9. Protect foods from insects, rodents, and other animals.

10. Use pure water.

World Health Organization

Contrary to popular opinion and media stories regarding the dangers to health from the food supply, illness does not usually result from the production or processing of food or from additives or trace levels of agricultural chemicals. Most foodborne disease results from pathogenic microorganisms that proliferate from the mishandling of food in food service establishments (e.g., restaurants) or in homes and other noncommercial situations. . . .

Few Americans grow a significant proportion of their own food. Overwhelmingly, consumers depend on the food industry, including producers (farmers, ranchers, fishermen), processors, distributors, retailers and food service operators, for what they eat. Food production is highly seasonal in most of the U.S.—if one wishes to eat only fresh, unprocessed food, one must pay to have the food transported great distances, perhaps from other countries. Alternatively, food produced seasonally must be processed or preserved to make it available throughout the year. The food industry plays a key role in either case, whether it be processing or distributing. Retailers and food service operators comprise the consumer-contact segment of the food industry—only when they have completed their tasks is the work of the industry done. Safety is all-important through every step from the farm to consumer consumption. . . .

Cost to Consumers of Mandating Greater "Safety"

It is important for consumers to realize that risk-free food cannot exist, and that any proposed increment of food safety will add significant cost to the food. For example, unopened canned food is "commercially sterile" (except those cans marked "keep refrigerated"), but most other foods contain many microorganisms. Many foods would be extremely unpalatable if they were processed for sterility. Even sterile foods might contain very small amounts of toxic substances such as mold toxins that were carried over from the raw material.

Some foods cannot be made safe as purchased. More effort will be made in regulating fish and seafoods, and this will result in some improvement. However, improved sanitation will not eliminate parasites from fish nor certain hazardous marine bacteria from shellfish. It is simply not possible to guarantee that fish and shellfish can safely be eaten raw. Additional government regulation of fish and seafoods may well enhance quality and improve sanitation, but no amount of time and effort (and added cost) will yield a risk-free product.

If consumers are unwilling to accept the risks they face eating under present circumstances, they may mandate changes in the system. Such changes might include more sanitation on farms and more rigorously controlled conditions in processing and distributing food. These would generally increase the retail cost of food and increase taxes for additional government enforcement activities. The consuming public must decide how much more they are willing to pay for slight reductions in risk. Those who are now eating very well might be willing to pay more, but those who cannot now afford to eat adequately would surely view the matter differently.

To attain the most food safety at a reasonable cost, it is important that consumers learn what the real food safety risks are, and accept some responsibility for their own actions in keeping food as safe as it was at the time of purchase. The U.S. food supply system is effective and working reasonably well. Any effort to improve it should be made very carefully, lest one result be that even more people in the U.S. cannot afford to eat adequately. Efforts by government and the food industry to educate the public about food safety are often viewed with suspicion. Still, more such efforts are needed, rather than less.

Most foodborne disease hazards are not caused by additives or pesticides, but are of microbial origin. *Regulatory activity should be allocated to reflect the fact that poor sanitation and preparation practices are more common in food service operations and in the home than in food processing establishments.* Government agencies must cooperate to achieve the best possible results with their always-limited resources. The food industry must continue to improve food safety, but the consuming public must understand that eating will never be risk-free and that self-protection requires understanding of and respect for the microbiological risks associated with eating.

> "Industry must not be allowed to
> shift responsibility to consumers for
> 'not cooking foods properly' when
> illness occurs."

CONSUMERS SHOULD DEMAND CHANGES IN THE FOOD INDUSTRY TO PREVENT FOOD-BORNE ILLNESSES

Nicols Fox

Nicols Fox is the author of *Spoiled: Why Our Food Is Making Us Sick and What We Can Do About It* (Basic Books, 1997; Penguin Books, 1998). In the following viewpoint, she maintains that outbreaks of food-borne illnesses reveal problems in the modern food production system. Many current practices in the way crops are grown, animals are raised, and food is processed and distributed increase the public's risks of contracting food-borne illnesses, she argues. Fox contends that consumers must go beyond basic safety measures (such as maintaining clean kitchens and cooking foods safely) and aggressively hold farmers, grocers, and companies that process food accountable for ensuring food safety.

As you read, consider the following questions:

1. How many cases of food-borne illnesses occur annually in the United States, according to Fox?
2. What has changed over the past 100 years in most people's relationship to the food they eat, according to the author?
3. What steps does Fox state consumers should take to increase the safety of their food?

Reprinted from "The Hidden Hazards in Our Food," by Nicols Fox, *Newsday*, August 31, 1997, by permission of the author.

The huge recall of hamburger from Hudson Meats in August 1997 is still sending shock waves through the American food industry. Hudson lost its biggest customer, the Burger King chain, and finally closed the Columbus, Neb., plant at the center of the 25-million pound recall after patties produced there were linked to 17 cases of *E. coli* O157:H7 contamination in Colorado.

Meat packers nationwide are now scrambling to introduce new safety standards and technologies, acknowledging that the practices that have devastated the Hudson company—notably the "reworking" of one day's leftover meat into the next day's output—are widespread in the industry.

A Food System out of Balance

American consumers greet all these developments, quite justifiably, with alarm and confusion. We have long taken for granted the notion that food producers can satisfy our appetites instantly, cleanly—and safely. This inadvertent glimpse behind the scenes of food processing seems a throwback to scandals stirred up by the publication of *The Jungle*, Upton Sinclair's muckraking novel about the Chicago stockyards in 1906.

But the real shock for American consumers is—or should be—that these abuses in meat processing constitute only one glancing symptom of a food-production system seriously out of balance. A few years ago an expert from the Centers for Disease Control in Atlanta suggested that probably everyone in the country has at least one case of foodborne disease a year. That was merely an educated guess, but it's a good bet that the bout of so-called stomach flu you had last year was probably related to something you ate.

A Widespread Problem

Although widespread lack of correct diagnosis and reporting of foodborne illnesses means that there are few hard numbers, scientific estimates as to the number of cases of illness in the United States each year range from 33 to 81 million. Many are mild illnesses from which individuals quickly recover. Other cases can be more serious, requiring medical treatment or hospitalization. But the microbes carried by food can kill. The United States Department of Agriculture puts the number of deaths from foodborne disease each year at 9,000. The annual costs generated by these illnesses may be as high as $22 billion.

Indeed, we learn almost weekly, it would seem, of food recalls, fresh outbreaks and bad news about foods we had assumed were safe. Around the country vocabularies are expanding as consumers learn about new pathogens (disease-causing microbes) with difficult names: Cyclospora, Cryptosporidium, Campylobacter, Listeria, Salmonella enteritidis and, of course, E. coli O157:H7. In the Washington, D.C., area 300 people were recently infected with a lingering illness from the parasite Cyclospora in products made from fresh basil. The same bug has been found two years running now on imported raspberries, causing widespread illnesses that spoiled wedding memories across the country. The vicious E. coli O157:H7, still mainly associated with ground beef, has now turned up in apple juice, alfalfa sprouts and mesclun salad mix. Some of our favorite foods, we are now forced to accept, can make us very sick or kill us.

In fact, foodborne disease is an old problem and ensuring safe food a historic challenge. Raw animal products have always had the potential to harbor disease-causing microorganisms and these same bugs, whether carried by hands or water or soil, can contaminate fruits, vegetables and other foods as well. Much human effort in times past went into keeping foods safe through drying, pickling, curing and, more recently, canning.

Our Relationship with Food

But a new generation of consumers has been lulled into complacency about food safety, placing too much trust in technology, food producers and federal regulators to guarantee a clean food supply. At the same time, the way we grow and transport vegetables, raise food animals, and process foods—even our consumption and cooking habits—have been transformed. We eat out more; we want convenience, novelty, year-round availability and cheapness. Food producers, for their part, want to increase efficiency and shelf-life and maximize profits. Intensive farming practices, which place virtually identical animals in close confines and subject them to physical and psychological stress, set the stage for animal infections. Economic pressures have led food producers to recycle even chicken litter as cattle feed, an unsavory practice if there ever was one.

We have in the last 100 years changed almost everything about our relationship to food, and the changes, not surprisingly, are making us sick. Each alteration has the potential to open the door to an emerging foodborne pathogen. Refrigeration is an effective food-safety tool, for instance, but microbes that like cool temperatures, such as Yersina and Listeria, which may be harbored by processed foods such as sliced meats and deli-salads, can have a field day in those chilly surroundings. Even simple changes can have huge, unexpected consequences. When a British company prepared hazelnut yogurt differently by using a sugar substitute, the new composition allowed *Clostridium botulinum* to grow. It was a mistake that led to 60 cases of botulism, a life-threatening infection.

Mass production and distribution, commonplace today, have also changed the nature of foodborne disease outbreaks. Once foodborne outbreaks were local—typically spoiled potato salad at a family reunion would make everyone who ate it sick. The outbreak and the food would be easy to identify. Today mass-produced and distributed foods can cause huge outbreaks that may go undetected because the illnesses they cause are widely scattered. In 1994 an ice-cream premix carried in tanker trucks that had previously carried eggs was made into enormous quantities of ice cream distributed across the country. Eventually the contaminated ice cream was found to have made 224,000 people ill in 48 states. The Hudson meat recall should come as no surprise when one contaminated cow can contaminate more than 16 tons of hamburger. When scraps of meat from hundreds of cows from several different countries meet in the huge grinders of giant processors, expect trouble.

WHAT CONSUMERS CAN DO

As consumers we can help protect ourselves by rethinking our whole relationship to food. We have forgotten, it seems, that eating is the single most important thing we do. The diminished importance we give to the family dinner and the carelessness with which we treat what we eat and how we prepare it is a factor in the rising tide of foodborne disease. Taking care to cook foods thoroughly and to avoid cross-contamination in the kitchen is a basic step, but it's only a beginning one. Industry must not be allowed to shift responsibility to consumers for "not cooking foods properly" when illness occurs. The roots of our thoroughly contaminated raw animal products, from chickens to eggs, begin with current rearing, slaughtering and processing practices that are encouraging and spreading pathogenic organisms. That "just cook it" line doesn't work in any case now that dangerous microbes are being found on salad greens and other foods we expect to eat raw.

I resent the number of traditional recipes that can no longer be safely made, from mousses to frostings to lemon meringue pie, as the danger from undercooked eggs increases. I am sad that shellfish are now too contaminated to eat raw. I am angry that rare hamburgers are no longer a sane option. These are incremental bites out of our food culture and tradition that are verging on the intolerable and the inexcusable. To look closely at how we raise, slaughter and process food animals and to trace the many countries and many hands and trucks our produce and processed foods pass through is to begin to understand why we are confronting a host of new infectious agents in what we eat.

Borgman. Reprinted by special permission of King Features Syndicate.

The marketplace and consumer demand are the most powerful tools for changing foods—but only if we, as consumers, have the information to act. There is a virtual wall of silence between food producers and consumers when it comes to safety. It is possible to produce *Salmonella*-free chickens, for instance, and Swedish consumers have the option of buying them. American producers need to clean up their act and offer American consumers the same option. Cleaner chickens will be more expensive, but it takes only one bout of *Salmonella* and a hospital stay to make it clear that saving a dollar or even $2 a pound on chicken is no saving at all.

There are cracks in the wall of silence. Legal Seafoods, a popular Boston restaurant chain, talks about food safety and what it takes to ensure clean, fresh fish on their placemats. The Country Hen, a Hubbardston, Mass., farm, tells its egg buyers what its chickens are fed and that they have been tested for *Salmonella enteritidis* and found negative. Farmers' markets, specializing in smaller-scale and organically farmed produce, are popping up all over the country.

MARKET ACCOUNTABILITY

The marketplace and consumer demand is the most powerful tool for changing foods—but only if we, as consumers, have the information to act. Food is too important to leave entirely to others. We should begin now to ask where produce comes from, what animals have eaten, whether *Salmonella* testing is going on regularly. In restaurants we can find the courage to send back the lasagna that arrives cool in the middle and ask that it be reheated. Buying locally grown produce in season is a good thing, because we can begin to develop a relationship with our food producers, and that, in turn, breeds accountability and responsibility into the exchange.

We must begin again with food. Restoring respect to the raising of food animals, to the harvesting of produce, to transportation and marketing, to food preparation and to eating together can begin incrementally to reduce foodborne disease. It won't happen overnight.

| "We can't address twenty-first century food safety problems with horse-and-buggy government programs."

INCREASED GOVERNMENT REGULATION IS NECESSARY TO PREVENT FOOD-BORNE ILLNESSES

Caroline Smith DeWaal

Caroline Smith DeWaal is director of food safety at the Center for Science in the Public Interest (CSPI), a nonprofit consumer advocacy organization. In the following viewpoint, DeWaal argues that the events of 1997 indicate that food-borne illnesses are a growing problem in the United States. She contends that the government regulatory apparatus charged with ensuring the safety of the nation's food supply is fragmented into multiple departments, resulting in inefficient and ineffective oversight. DeWaal calls for legislative reforms that would give greater regulatory powers to the government and centralize its food safety operations in one agency.

As you read, consider the following questions:

1. Why are outbreaks of food-borne illnesses underreported, according to DeWaal?
2. What are some of the government agencies that share responsibility for inspecting food, according to DeWaal?
3. What problem is revealed by Sue Doneth's question about who was responsible for her daughter's illness, according to the author?

Excerpted from Caroline Smith DeWaal's remarks to the National Press Club, November 19, 1997 (full text available at http://www.cspinet.org/reports/safefood.htm).

It is unlikely that safe food will be a hallmark of 1997. In fact, it seems that almost weekly there is another major food poisoning episode somewhere in the nation. In November 1997, it was Salmonella-contaminated stuffed hams at a church dinner that killed two and infected over 700. In October, it was hepatitis A from a Michigan delicatessen that killed one and sickened dozens. In August, an outbreak of E. coli O157:H7 from beef patties resulted in the largest-ever meat recall. [Hudson Foods agreed to recall 25 million pounds of ground beef.]

Since 1990, food poisoning outbreaks have become commonplace and the types of foods that are contaminated seem to be growing. While we all know that meat, poultry and seafood are high-risk foods, we don't expect to find Salmonella on cantaloupes, tomatoes, alfalfa sprouts and in orange juice; or harmful E. coli in apple cider and on lettuce and alfalfa sprouts; or even parasites, like Cyclospora and Cryptosporidum, on raspberries, lettuce, and in apple cider; or hepatitis A on strawberries served in the school lunch program. Yet, such unexpected outbreaks are occurring with disturbing frequency.

These examples are a few of the 26 outbreaks linked to fruits and vegetables since 1990 that CSPI has identified. These outbreaks alone involve over 5,000 cases of illness. And they represent just the tip of the iceberg. Fruits and vegetables are rarely the first food suspected when people become ill from Salmonella, E. coli, or other pathogens, so it takes a lot of detective work to track down a fruit or vegetable culprit in a food poisoning outbreak. Many outbreaks like these go unrecognized and many, many victims remain uncounted.

Regardless of what consumers thought before, one thing is becoming apparent. Food poisoning is not just a bellyache anymore. The causes of food-borne illness seem to be tougher and less treatable than before.

E. Coli O157:H7

For example, when we talk about the bacterium E. coli O157:H7, we are talking about a devastating human pathogen. First identified in 1982, it is now the single largest cause of renal failure among American children. Just a few bacteria can leave a child hanging between life and death for weeks on end, while the parents hope and pray. There is no cure yet. Doctors support the children through blood transfusions and kidney dialysis, which can be very tough for a little child. Thankfully, not all infected children die but the survivors often have lifelong effects from the illness. And children aren't the only victims. It causes severe illnesses and deaths in adults and the elderly as well.

E. coli O157:H7 has certainly taken its place in the rogues' gallery of food-borne bacteria. Some of the trends that we are watching with E. coli include (1) how many strains other than O157:H7 will be found to cause severe human illness and (2) how many animals, other than cattle, serve as carriers. Our long-term ability to control this pathogen will depend on the answer to these questions and others.

OTHER DANGEROUS PATHOGENS

Cyclospora, the parasite that raspberries made famous, can also cause a devastating illness if left untreated. While not fatal, it can cause weeks of extreme fatigue and result in consumers losing twenty or more pounds. During the 1996 outbreak traced to imported raspberries, it took doctors weeks to recognize the condition because it is so rare in the United States. At least it was rare, until Guatemalan raspberries made clear the full implications of unrestricted world trade.

A SINGLE AGENCY MEANS SAFER FOOD

Today, multiple agencies—including the U.S. Department of Agriculture (USDA), the Food and Drug Administration (FDA), and the Environmental Protection Agency (EPA)—are in charge of ensuring a safe food supply. Twelve different federal agencies and 35 different laws govern food safety and inspection functions. With so many bureaucrats in the kitchen, breakdowns can and do occur.

A single agency with one mission—ensuring that the food we eat is safe—would reduce the risk that contaminated food could make its way from the farm to the fork. Bottom line, it would mean safer food.

Center for Science in the Public Interest, "CSPI's Recipe for Safe Food: A Campaign to Clean Up America's Food Supply," 1998.

There are many unanswered questions about the Cyclospora parasite, even among US scientists. Those studying and treating food-borne diseases in Third World countries are the best experts. Now we are waiting to see if Cyclospora has somehow gotten a toe hold in the United States, which would mean we might see cases cropping up without any link to imported produce. The other trend worth watching is whether other disease-causing agents common in foreign countries gain entry to the US through our newly expanding food imports.

Another emerging hazard is Salmonella typhimurium DT104. This strain of Salmonella originated in Europe and has recently appeared in the US. It is found in meat products, particularly beef, but cases in Europe have been linked to other foods as well. DT104 causes severe cases of food poisoning, which frequently require hospitalization. DT104 is also resistant to many types of antibiotics that are used to treat patients with the most severe symptoms. And the news from Europe is that the strain can develop additional antibiotic resistance very quickly. DT104 is truly an emerging "super bug," which draws into question the widespread use of antibiotics in animal husbandry. It would be a travesty if the use of antibiotics to speed the growth of livestock meant more severe food poisoning illnesses for humans and more treatment-resistant illnesses like Salmonella typhimurium DT104.

RATIONALIZING GOVERNMENT RESOURCES

Following the Hudson beef recall in August 1997, members of Congress started to look for solutions to address the food safety problems that we are facing. Representative Vic Fazio (D-CA) and Senators Richard Durbin (D-IL) and Robert Torricelli (D-NJ) introduced the *Safe Food Act* of 1997, which would direct the President to create the independent Food Safety Administration, formed from numerous agencies which currently share food safety responsibilities [the legislation had not passed as of May 1998].

Making more effective use of existing government resources is an obvious solution that CSPI started promoting in the spring of 1997, together with the families of Safe Table Our Priority (S.T.O.P.), a victim support and advocacy organization. Today food safety functions are spread out between numerous federal agencies:

- The United States Department of Agriculture (USDA) employs 7000 inspectors at its Food Safety and Inspection Service who visit 6500 meat, poultry and egg products plants.
- The Food and Drug Administration (FDA) employs fewer than 700 inspectors to visit 53,000 food processing plants.
- The Environmental Protection Agency approves pesticide residue levels on food but FDA enforces them.
- The Centers for Disease Control and Prevention (CDC) collects food poisoning data from the states and conducts outbreak investigations.
- The Agricultural Research Service funds food safety research.

- As many as 15 agencies do other tasks, including seafood inspection at the Department of Commerce and egg inspection at USDA's Agricultural Marketing Service. Both of these functions are funded by the respective industries.

When S.T.O.P. and CSPI first identified the trend in E. coli outbreaks linked to lettuce in 1996, we discovered that there was no place to go in the federal government to address the problem. USDA's food safety branch, which is the agency with the most experience with the harmful E. coli strain, doesn't regulate fruits and vegetables. FDA regulates fruits and vegetables but not at the farm level. No one regulates manure, which was the likely source for contamination.

Clearly this has to change. The future challenges are too great. We can't address twenty-first century food safety problems with horse-and-buggy government programs. With so much fragmentation, sometimes nothing gets done. One agency doesn't have responsibility. Another doesn't have the research money. A third is too busy addressing other pressing public health problems.

REFORMING THE SYSTEM

After over 200 students and employees in a Michigan school system came down with hepatitis A in 1997 that was traced to contaminated strawberries served in the school lunch, Sue Doneth, the mother of a 10-year-old victim called me and asked "Who didn't do their job?" She wanted to track down the person in the federal government who had the duty to protect her daughter from those contaminated berries. Today, there is no single person or agency who failed Sue Doneth. Today, the whole system fails that mother's test.

With dangerous new pathogens entering the food supply, we need government programs ready, willing and able to tackle these challenges. Representative Fazio said recently that the new independent Food Safety Administration he is proposing "will have a single mission: to ensure that American consumers are eating safe food." The Food Safety Administration would be a wish come true for many American parents.

| "A single food agency bent on the needless expansion of enforcement authority . . . would be a disaster."

INCREASED GOVERNMENT REGULATION IS NOT NECESSARY TO PREVENT FOOD-BORNE ILLNESSES

John R. Cady

Some congressional leaders and other commentators have argued that the government's system of food regulation is divided into too many separate agencies, none of which have the overall authority or capacity to adequately provide safeguards for America's food supply. These critics advocate the creation of a central government food regulation agency. In the following viewpoint, John R. Cady argues that such a reform would do little to improve food safety. He contends that the existing regulatory system, in which food companies and various regulatory agencies cooperate in preventing unsafe foods from reaching consumers, has been effective because food manufacturers and sellers have a vested interest in preserving food safety. Cady is president of the National Food Processors Association, a scientific and trade association that conducts research and government lobbying for member companies in the food processing industry. The following viewpoint is excerpted from a speech he delivered to the Mid-America Food Processors Association in December 1997.

As you read, consider the following questions:

1. According to Cady, why do food companies have a vested interest in food safety?
2. What abuses of power might result from the creation of a "food czar," according to the author?

Excerpted from John R. Cady's speech to the Mid-America Food Processors Association, December 1, 1997 (full text available at http://www.nfpa-food.org/Speech/midamerica.html).

I sometimes worry that I talk so much about government regulation and legislation and the impact it has on our industry that what I say falls on deaf ears and is treated like death and taxes.

It is imperative, however, that all of us understand what a critical impact food agency regulatory actions and legislative proposals have in determining the food industry's marketplace stability and competitiveness.

Today I would like to focus on one issue that I think will have a strong impact on our industry—food safety and, in particular, the proposal to create a single U.S. food safety agency.

A Call for a "Food Czar"

In November 1997, a handful of Democratic Senators and Congressmen unveiled a proposal to merge all federal agencies responsible for our food safety system into a single entity, led by a "food czar."

Right now there are, in effect, two separate food safety systems in America—one system for meat and poultry, managed by the U.S. Department of Agriculture (USDA), and one system for other foods, directed by the Food and Drug Administration (FDA). In addition, the Environmental Protection Agency (EPA) regulates the use of pesticides on foods, and the Centers for Disease Control and Prevention (CDC) monitors foodborne illness.

To the casual observer, as well as to advocacy groups, merging food agencies under one roof seems to make sense. Single food agency proponents like to use the example of pizza. Cheese pizza falls under the exclusive jurisdiction of FDA, but if pepperoni or sausage are added, then USDA steps in. And states can add to the confusion as well. While federal law provides national uniformity for some food labeling requirements—such as the information on the "Nutrition Facts" panel—any state can pile on its own requirements.

Certainly, it could be said that there is a need for greater simplicity—streamlining—and uniformity of regulatory requirements. But before Congress rushes to judgment on the issue of a single food agency, it needs to answer an important question: Does America really need a food czar?

The Existing System Works Well

Scientific experts and policy makers alike have repeatedly called our food supply the world's safest. There are two primary reasons why our existing system works so well.

First, food companies have a vested interest in the safety of their products. Any company that takes unnecessary chances on the safety of its product just will not be in business for very long. Second, the current food safety system is based on a mutual commitment to food safety by the companies and the regulatory agencies. Politics must not enter into the food safety process.

Some "consumer advocates" point to recent reports of food-borne illness outbreaks as evidence the system is broken. In reality, the number of outbreaks reported is increasing because our monitoring and reporting has vastly improved. The fact of the matter is that there is no such thing as a "zero risk" food safety system. Mother Nature just won't stand still. Nothing is absolute in our business, no matter how good we are. But common sense can still go far in managing foodborne illness.

Even if our food safety system isn't broken, could we make it better by creating a new single food agency, led by a national food czar? The answer is: No way.

EXPANDING BUREAUCRACY

Granted, a single food agency—built on the strengths of the current system and focused on sound science, commonsense regulation, and national uniformity—could strengthen our food safety system. But can that really happen—in Washington? I think not.

A single food agency bent on the needless expansion of enforcement authority and an agenda that goes beyond the government's current mission would be a disaster, and nothing but a new level of bureaucracy—with new rules, new forms, and more inspection—would come from this new agency. Moving from today's system to a single agency would not be easy. The current players, from FDA to EPA, perform very different tasks for very different products and purposes, and will want to maintain their existing influence over our industry.

THE GOVERNMENT CANNOT MAKE GUARANTEES

Most people desperately want to believe that someone else will look out for them. We'd like to believe that just as we can drive over a bridge and not have to get out of the car and check it for safety, we can be equally confident that the government has declared our food safe. But it's not that easy.

Michael T. Osterholm, *Newsweek*, September 1, 1997.

Today, I see little in total costs that a single agency would eliminate, and even less would be saved from duplicated efforts. I have yet in twenty years in Washington to see a savings of real dollars that resulted from mergers of government operations under the guise of reducing duplication of efforts.

Another hurdle would be Congressional jurisdiction. Right now, two House and two Senate committees share jurisdiction over the nation's food safety system. Each takes rightful pride in its expertise and role in the process and would be hard pressed to relinquish its responsibilities. This is a major hurdle to be overcome—perhaps the largest issue to be addressed.

TOO MUCH POWER IN ONE PERSON

But these mechanical impediments pale against the larger question: Is it really wise to hand over so much power to a single individual—especially a politically appointed person—to direct the nation's entire food safety system? It is not difficult to imagine this powerful new position becoming a lightning rod for all sorts of political mischief. A food czar dedicated to using the food safety system to build support for a political agenda could severely harm our food safety system, put real fear in consumers, and imperil jobs built on U.S. food exports.

The National Highway Traffic Safety Administration provides an example of how a safety agency can impose itself between consumers and industry. At the baggage claim section of Washington's Dulles International Airport, travelers are treated to a large advertisement inviting consumers who are troubled by vehicle defects to call an 800-number.

Perhaps there is a demonstrated need for this type of a government role involving auto manufacturers—but for foods? I think not. Yet that would be the ultimate achievement for a single food agency and the advocacy groups who work on the premises of fear and total government involvement in our lives.

Imagine a federal food safety agency advertisement inviting consumers to call the government over a concern regarding food safety "defects." Where would the government draw the line? Where would the press draw the line? How would consumers react to what they read about such "defects" and what would the food industry have to do to maintain government and consumer confidence in our food safety systems?

A food czar, armed with the powers being proposed by some members of Congress, could singlehandedly force a company to recall a product and impose huge civil money penalties, and could put CEOs in jail for food safety violations.

Taken a step further, the czar could easily use that unbridled authority to raise money for his or her agency through fines, destroying branded and private label products, and putting a company and its workers out of business altogether for the slightest reason—with no recourse if the government made a mistake. Of course, we all know that the government doesn't make mistakes!

As you know, government agencies continually justify their existence by action, and we—the food industry—would be "the object of their affection" in this regard.

The advantages of a system with effective checks and balances must be protected against the very real dangers of consolidating so much power into the hands of a single, independent, Cabinet-level office. . . .

We can—and should—always strive for improvement, but creating a food czar isn't the way to go about it. . . .

THE INDUSTRY'S ROLE IN THE DEBATE

Our nation's food safety efforts must be based on sound, scientific policy, not politics and fear-mongering by our nation's leaders.

As the debate continues on the value of a single food agency, or on expanding FDA's and USDA's enforcement powers, or on other food safety related issues, our industry must lead the discussion. No one has a more vested interest in food safety than you: the processor. What's more, no one knows more about food safety—and how to produce foods safely—than you: the processor.

When it comes to examining or reorganizing the system by which food safety is assured in our country, you, the processor, should lead—not follow. Processors and their associations must actively be involved to protect our industry from the politics of food safety.

I "Irradiation can save our food."

IRRADIATION CAN PREVENT FOOD-BORNE DISEASES

Richard Rhodes

Richard Rhodes is an author whose works include *Deadly Feasts: Tracking the Secrets of a Terrifying New Plague* and *The Making of the Atomic Bomb*. In the following viewpoint, he argues that irradiation— the bombarding of food with gamma rays to kill disease agents such as bacteria and fungi—is a potent technological solution to the problem of food-borne illnesses. He contends that irradiation, for instance, could have prevented the recall and subsequent destruction of 25 million pounds of ground meat produced by a processing plant owned by Hudson Foods in August 1997 after samples were found to be contaminated with dangerous bacteria. Rhodes asserts that irrational public fears of radiation and the opposition of some environmental groups have prevented food processors from utilizing this technology, thereby causing needless suffering and death from preventable food-borne diseases.

As you read, consider the following questions:

1. How long has the technology for food irradiation been available, according to Rhodes?
2. What potential disease agents found in food can be killed by irradiation, according to the author?
3. According to Rhodes, why has irradiation seen only limited use in the United States?

It's a good rule of thumb that technological solutions work better than increased regulation. Before 1920, thousands of babies died annually in New York and other large American cities from drinking contaminated milk. The solution wasn't more Federal dairy inspectors or a merger of Government agencies. It was pasteurization.

The solution to the problem of food poisoning—whether the food involved is hamburger, strawberries, raspberries, cider or some other product susceptible to bacterial contamination—has been sitting on the shelf for most of 40 years while hundreds of thousands of Americans have been sickened and thousands have died. It is the equivalent of pasteurization, and its neglect is a disgrace.

FOOD IRRADIATION

The technology is food irradiation. The Army pioneered its development beginning in 1943, and it has since passed into commercial application in some 40 countries, including limited use in the United States.

Irradiation uses gamma rays from a solid radioactive source to disrupt the DNA of, and thus to kill, noxious bacteria, parasites, mold and fungus in and on agricultural products. Gamma rays are similar to microwaves and X-rays.

Irradiation doesn't make food radioactive, nor does it noticeably change taste, texture or appearance. Depending on dose and on whether the food is packaged to prevent recontamination, irradiation can retard spoilage, kill germs or even completely preserve. The World Health Organization, the American Medical Association and the American Veterinary Medical Association all endorse the process.

The Food and Drug Administration (FDA) has approved irradiation of pork, poultry, fruits, vegetables, spices and grains, although its use remains limited. Most imported spices are preserved with irradiation. Tropical fruits like mango and papaya from Hawaii are treated to kill exotic pests. Irradiated chicken is served in hospitals in the Southeast. Astronauts aboard the space shuttle eat irradiated food, including steak.

PREVENTING ILLNESSES

Food irradiation would have prevented the illnesses caused by contaminated hamburger from Hudson Foods and the several deaths linked to Jack in the Box restaurants in the Northwest in 1993. It could kill the salmonella that infects up to 60 percent of the poultry and eggs sold in the United States; the deadly mutant E. coli strain O157:H7, which the Centers for Disease Control and Prevention have characterized as a major emerging infectious disease; and such ugly stowaways as beef tapeworms, fish parasites and the nematodes that cause trichinosis in pork.

ENDORSEMENTS OF IRRADIATION

"The benefits of food irradiation are overwhelming," says Richard Lechowich, director of the National Center for Food Safety and Technology at the Illinois Institute of Technology. High-energy radiation kills critters that live in or on food, including the deadly E. coli O157:H7 bacterium and the salmonella and campylobacter species of bacteria found in most uncooked chicken and turkey. "Widespread irradiation of poultry alone in this country could prevent thousands of illnesses and hundreds of deaths every year," concurs Douglas Archer, former deputy director of the Center for Food Safety and Applied Nutrition at the U.S. Food and Drug Administration (FDA).

A major benefit of irradiation is that it can occur after food is packaged and sealed to kill any organisms that may have contaminated the food between production line and plate. "We don't live in a perfect world where we always detect E. coli on a processing line, and where everyone washes their hands and cutting boards and cooks meat and poultry to the proper temperature," says Christine Bruhn, director of the Center for Consumer Research at the University of California at Davis. Food irradiation is like an air bag in a car, she says. Both offer an extra measure of safety in case of carelessness or accident.

More than 40 countries share this view, having authorized irradiation for everything from apples in China and frog legs in France to rice in Mexico, raw pork sausages in Thailand, and wheat in Canada. Irradiation has been endorsed not only by the U.N. World Health Organization and the Food and Agriculture Organization, but also by the U.S. Food and Drug Administration, the American Medical Association, and the American Public Health Association, among others.

P.J. Skerrett, *Technology Review*, November/December 1997.

Yet the new meat inspection system now being phased in by the United States Department of Agriculture does not even mention, much less mandate, irradiation. Neither Agriculture Secretary Dan Glickman nor the Food and Drug Administration invoked food irradiation as a solution to the Hudson Foods situation, preferring instead to press for destruction of 25 million pounds of meat that could have been made edible with the technique.

A petition for authorization to irradiate red meat has languished at the FDA since 1994. [The FDA approved the irradiation of red meat in December 1997.] Several states, including New York, have responded to pressure from citizen groups by either banning or imposing a moratorium on the sale of irradiated food without reviewing scientific evidence of the technology's safety and value.

IRRATIONAL FEARS

Why the gap between promise and application? Because food irradiation—like cancer treatment, medical diagnostics, sterilization of medical disposables, aircraft maintenance and many other technologies—uses radioactivity, which Americans have been taught to fear. Commercial irradiators use metallic cesium-137 or cobalt-60 as sources of gamma radiation in heavily shielded processing plants; when the radioactive sources are not being used to sanitize food, they are stored safely underground.

Some anti-nuclear and environmental groups have campaigned against food irradiation, even imagining a conspiracy among the Food and Drug Administration, the World Health Organization and the nuclear power industry to use the process to dispose of nuclear waste.

Similarly fanatic resistance plagued the introduction of vaccination, water chlorination, pasteurization and fluoridation—comparable technologies that have reduced disease and saved millions of lives. The unsupported fears of the Luddite opposition are making people suffer needlessly.

Mr. Glickman has said that the Hudson Foods case highlights the need to better educate the public on how to prepare food properly, but we can't all become sterile technicians at home.

Thermometers won't protect us from E. coli–contaminated alfalfa sprouts. Public health has been a primary responsibility of Government for more than a century. Inspection and testing alone, however responsibly applied, can never assure consumer safety where invisible pathogens are concerned.

Pasteurization saved the babies. Irradiation can save our food.

"Instead of simplistically treating food with radioactive cobalt, a systematic attack is needed to minimize levels of dangerous microorganisms."

IRRADIATION IS NOT THE SOLUTION TO THE PROBLEM OF FOOD-BORNE DISEASES

Part I: Michael Colby, interviewed by Ros Davidson,
Part II: Michael F. Jacobson

In the following viewpoint, Michael Colby and Michael F. Jacobson question whether food irradiation is an appropriate method of preventing food-borne illnesses. In Part I, Colby, the director of Food & Water, an advocacy group that opposes food irradiation, is interviewed by writer Ros Davidson. He argues that irradiation technology is untested and that irradiated foods are potentially hazardous to a person's health. In Part II, Jacobson contends that irradiation is a costly solution that should only be used as a last resort. Jacobson is president of the Center for Science in the Public Interest, a consumer advocacy organization.

As you read, consider the following questions:

1. What concerns does Colby express about the FDA's ability to determine the safety of irradiation
2. Why are consumers hesitant to buy irradiated food, according to Jacobson?
3. What policy alternatives to radiation does Jacobson propose?

I

Ros Davidson: *What is your concern about irradiated red meat?*

Michael Colby: Food & Water is opposed to the irradiation of all food products on the basis of the health concerns, environmental impact and nuclear proliferation surrounding this technology. The health issue is potentially quite serious. When you expose food to the equivalent of 10 million to 70 million chest X-rays. . . .

Seventy million? Did I hear you correctly?

Yes, I'm giving you an equivalency in terms of radiation: 70 million. Irradiating food is not like exposing it to the volume of radiation in an airport luggage scanner or a regular X-ray. It is equivalent to 10 million to 70 million chest X-rays. Ten million—which is 100,000 "rads," the unit that radiation is measured in—is what's approved for fruit and vegetables, and up to 70 million range is the approved dose for frozen meat products, which is 700,000 rads. And a chest X-ray is .01 rad.

Concerns About Food Safety

The irradiation is on foodstuffs though, not our bodies. And hasn't irradiation been approved for chicken since 1990 and on fruits, vegetables and spices since 1986? (The government requires that irradiated foods be clearly labeled.)

First of all, food irradiation has never been proven safe. There are no long-term, multi-generational studies. So the meat industry and the government have completely neglected their responsibility of proving its safety.

I gather you're concerned, especially for children, about irradiated foods containing radiolytic compounds. What are they?

When you expose food to radiation, you create radiolytic products, which are products that result from the process of irradiation. For example, when you expose red meat to irradiation at the approved doses, you create benzene in the meat. Benzene is a very, very potent carcinogen. The government is spending tens of millions of dollars to try to get it out of the vapors of gasoline, and now we're putting it in the red meat supply. If there's one molecule of benzene created in the red meat and that molecule gets into the human body, that's enough to cause cancer. It's not enough to argue that it's only a small amount, so don't worry about it. I say look at the cancer rate in this country—I think we've had enough of the public policy that says, "It's only a small carcinogenic insult so don't worry about it."

So what about the impact on children?

In fact, one of the only studies on human beings that exists was done on children in India who were fed irradiated wheat.

The researchers found that children who were fed stored and freshly irradiated wheat developed chromosomal abnormalities in their blood known as "polyploidy." Many scientists believe that polyploidy is a precursor to leukemia and other forms of cancer. The study was done in 1976 and published in the *American Journal of Clinical Nutrition*.

But isn't it being accepted as the only way to make food safer?

It's an unnecessary technology—we know how to decrease levels of e-coli without taking on the risks of added carcinogens and a reduced vitamin and mineral content. Let's address the causes of what allows these microorganisms to flourish. Exposing dirty food to nuclear waste is not somehow going to make it safe.

How much is the vitamin content of food changed by irradiation?

It depends on the food. It can be as high as 60 percent, depending on the food and the dose. Radiation-sensitive vitamins are vitamin C, D, E, K and A.

Do you have other concerns apart from irradiation causing carcinogens?

The primary concern is the introduction of new chemicals, some of which are known to be carcinogenic. Another is the depletion of nutrients and vitamins. Another is the environmental implications. If this is truly going to be the solution to a contaminated industrial food supply, we're going to need a nuclear infrastructure in this country of at least 500 to 750 new nuclear facilities.

QUESTIONING THE FDA

When the Food and Drug Administration (FDA) approved this, many scientists were quoted in the press saying this technology is safe. How do you account for that?

Well, the coverage has been unconscionable.

But what might the scientists be basing that view on?

They're no doubt basing it on risk assessment and a backward form of thinking in terms of problem-solving, which is: Grab the latest gimmick rather than trying to look at causes and speak about prevention. The coverage of this issue has been so shallow. You don't hear anything about nuclear accidents that have happened at the food irradiation facilities in this country; or about carcinogenic properties, which are known; or about why we're allowing the causes—not least of which are the meat monopolies that control the meat industry—to flourish. Why do five food corporations control 92 percent of the meat industry? That's a problem, particularly when they're vertically integrated—when they control the factory farms, the filthy slaughtering and processing facilities, the wholesaling—and they're concerned primarily with profit, not safety.

Don't other nations use irradiation? The World Health Organization has generally approved the procedure, as has the American Medical Association.

It's approved in 40 countries, but it's used very, very sparingly. Just like here, it's been approved since 1986, but very few foods are actually irradiated. In fact, the world's leader for irradiated food, probably responsible for 90 percent of irradiated food, is China. The other major leader is the former Soviet Union. There's kind of a shell-game going on worldwide in which Europe and Asia say the U.S. is eating the stuff up and we're falling behind, and the U.S. says, Asia is using it, and we're falling behind. There's no truth in that. We've done surveys in the major countries that have approval and found they're a lot like the U.S.—they have approved a lot of uses for it, but they're not using it.

Is that mostly because consumers just don't buy it?

Yes, there's enormous citizen opposition to the idea of exposing food products that we require for health and well-being to nuclear waste products.

Then what did the FDA base its approval on?

At one point in the 1980s, over half of the drugs the FDA had approved were eventually recalled, in some cases because the agency realized that the drugs caused more problems than they cured. The FDA approved breast implants. The FDA and other federal agencies approved DDT in the past. To say that the FDA has approved it doesn't really mean a lot. One, the people at the FDA are human beings, so they're fallible. Two, it's a political agency. The head of the FDA and many of its top deputies are political appointees, not scientists.

I encourage the American people to look at the data that the FDA based its approvals on and talk to scientists-epidemiologists, toxicologists or cancer researchers who have looked at the data and are beside themselves over the approval, namely the head of the FDA's own food irradiation panel in the 1980s, Dr. Marcia Van Gemert. She's a toxicologist and was the head of the committee that looked at hundreds of FDA studies on irradiated foods in the 1980s. In 1993, she came out with a statement saying that the studies were inadequate to evaluate the toxicity of irradiated foods.

Or talk to Dr. Donald Louria, head of the Department of Preventive Medicine at the New Jersey Medical School in Newark, N.J., who looked at the same FDA studies. In some of the studies, he saw nutritional problems, still births, tumors, methodology that was borderline fraudulent by including nutritional supplements in the diets of animals fed irradiated food, supposedly to offset nutritional inadequacies. There were all kinds of things going wrong that were basically ignored by the FDA. This isn't just Michael Colby saying this. This isn't just any health food advocate. These are scientists who have studied the data that this approval is based on and found it flawed.

II

Do consumers want irradiated food? Advocates say "yes" and propose zapping everything from basil to burgers with cobalt-60 to kill E. coli and other germs. We need to stem the epidemic of food-poisoning outbreaks, but irradiation should be the method of last resort, not first.

For starters, constructing countless new irradiation facilities would take years and would be extraordinarily costly. Also, the radioactive chemicals in those facilities could endanger workers and contaminate the environment.

Many consumers are hesitant to buy foods bearing a notice "treated with irradiation." They are concerned about vitamin losses, impaired taste and the safety of the new technology. And people prefer food that is really clean to food contaminated with fecal matter, even if it is germ-free. . . .

ALTERNATIVE SOLUTIONS

Instead of simplistically treating food with radioactive cobalt, a systematic attack is needed to minimize levels of dangerous microorganisms. Then, to buttress industry's efforts, the government should be given power to recall tainted food and fine companies that endanger lives. . . . Also:

- Farmers should raise livestock in ways that prevent the spread of germs, not encourage infections through overcrowding and other factory-farming methods.
- Sloppy slaughterhouses—where one germ-ridden carcass may contaminate others—should be upgraded or shut down.
- Hamburger makers should be required to test their products for bacteria and be barred from adding today's leftovers to tomorrow's patties.
- Supermarkets and restaurants should be required to maintain careful protections against food contamination.
- Sensible new technologies should be introduced: washing chicken carcasses in benign disinfectants, cleansing beef carcasses with steam, inoculating livestock with safe bacteria to crowd out dangerous ones.

That kind of comprehensive approach should provide the greatest protection at the lowest cost. If that fails to bring food poisoning under control, then, and only then, should we irradiate.

PERIODICAL BIBLIOGRAPHY

The following articles have been selected to supplement the diverse views presented in this chapter. Addresses are provided for periodicals not indexed in the *Readers' Guide to Periodical Literature*, the *Alternative Press Index*, the *Social Sciences Index*, or the *Index to Legal Periodicals and Books*.

Sean F. Altekruse and David L. Swerdlow	"The Changing Epidemiology of Foodborne Diseases," *American Journal of the Medical Sciences*, January 1996. Available from the Department of Veterans Affairs Medical Center, Medical Service (111), 1500 E. Woodrow Wilson Dr., Jackson, MS 39216.
John Berlau	"Care for a Rare, Irradiated Burger?" *Insight*, September 22, 1997. Available from 3600 New York Ave. NE, Washington, DC 20002.
Dick Boland	"Eat, Drink, and Be Sick," *Conservative Chronicle*, September 24, 1997. Available from PO Box 37077, Boone, IA 50037-0077.
Alexander Cockburn	"Enforce Sanitation Standards That Work," *Liberal Opinion*, October 6, 1997. Available from PO Box 880, Vinton, IA 52349-0880.
Bill Grierson	"Food Safety Through the Ages," *Priorities*, vol. 9, no.3, 1997. Available from 1995 Broadway, 2nd Fl., New York, NY 10023-5860.
Tom Morganthau	"E. Coli Alert," *Newsweek*, September 1, 1997.
Michael T. Osterholm	"No Magic Bullet," *Newsweek*, September 1, 1997.
P.J. Skerrett	"Food Irradiation: Will It Keep the Doctor Away?" *Technology Review*, November/December 1997.
Don Sloan	"The Politics Behind the Endangered Food Supply," *Political Affairs*, January 1998.
Amanda Spake	"O Is for Outbreak," *U.S. News & World Report*, November 24, 1997.
Elizabeth M. Whelan	"Safe Meat: There Is a Better Way," *Wall Street Journal*, August 26, 1997.

GLOSSARY

AIDS   Acquired immunodeficiency syndrome; the name used to describe a variety of often fatal illnesses brought about by **HIV**-induced suppression of the **immune system.**

antibodies   Compounds that are produced by the body to destroy foreign substances, including **pathogens.**

arbovirus   A family of **viruses** transmitted by insects; includes the causative agents of dengue fever, yellow fever, and encephalitis.

bacteria   Microscopic single-celled organisms. Many are harmless or live in symbiotic relationships with humans. Others are **pathogens** that cause a number of infectious diseases including cholera, typhoid fever, and tetanus.

BSL   Biosafety Level; classification system for **microorganisms** used to set safety procedures in U.S. government laboratories. Levels range from BSL 1 to BSL 4. BSL 1 is the least hazardous and refers to familiar **microorganisms** not known to cause disease in healthy human adults. BSL 4 agents are the most dangerous, consisting of exotic, possibly airborne agents that carry a high risk of life-threatening disease and have no known vaccine or cure. BSL 4 requires maximum safety and isolation procedures and containment equipment.

Centers for Disease Control and Prevention (CDC)   Formerly called the Centers for Disease Control, a federal government agency charged with tracking and preventing the spread of **infectious diseases** in the United States.

cryptosporidium   A **parasite** found in contaminated food and water.

DNA   Deoxyribonucleic acid; the substance from which chromosomes inside the cell nucleus are formed. In most organisms **DNA** sequences comprise the genes—the biochemical information necessary for the development and life of the organism.

DPT   Vaccine for diptheria, pertussis (whooping cough), and tetanus.

Ebola   An extremely lethal **filovirus** from the African tropics whose origins are unknown; closely related to the **Marburg** virus. Three subtypes have been classified: *Ebola Zaire, Ebola Sudan,* and *Ebola Reston.*

E. coli   *Escherichia coli;* a class of **bacteria** that is found in the intestines of all animals and humans; some types, including type O157:H7, cause disease.

epidemic   A widespread outbreak of disease that affects many humans.

epidemiology   The study of diseases and their spread.

Food and Drug Administration (FDA)   The government agency responsible for testing drugs for safety and enforcing federal food laws.

filovirus   A family of **viruses** that includes the **Ebola** and **Marburg** viruses**.**

hantavirus   A **virus** spread by rodents that was responsible for several human fatalities in America's Southwest in the 1990s.

herd immunity   The concept that 100 percent immunization rates are not necessary to eradicate disease because if enough people are vaccinated the disease will not find enough **hosts** to spread.

Hib   The **bacteria** *Haemophilus influenzae* type b; a common cause of bacterial meningitis among children until vaccinations for **Hib** were introduced in 1987.

HIV   Human immunodeficiency virus, a **retrovirus** widely believed to cause **AIDS.** Two strains have been identified: HIV-1 and HIV-2.

host   An organism that serves as a home to and food supply for a **parasite**, such as a **virus.**

immune system   The cells of the body that protect against **infectious diseases** by producing **antibodies** that attack **pathogens.**

infectious disease   A disease that is caused by a **pathogen** and can be spread from one individual to others.

Marburg   A relative of the **Ebola** virus first documented in Marburg, Germany, in 1967; outbreaks have also occurred in South Africa and Kenya.

microorganism   A small form of life visible only through a microscope; includes **bacteria**, **viruses,** fungi, and some **parasites**.

pandemic   A worldwide **epidemic.**

parasite   An organism that lives in or on another individual (the **host**), often to the **host's** detriment.

pathogen   A **microorganism**, such as a **virus**, **bacterium**, or protozoan, that causes disease.

plasmid   A loop of **DNA** in **bacteria** that can be transferred between different **bacteria**; it often contains genes for antibiotic resistance, toxins, and the ability to invade **host** cells.

retrovirus   A kind of **virus** that replicates by copying its **RNA** onto a **host** cell's **DNA.**

RNA   Ribonucleic acid; long-chained molecules. In most organisms **RNA** serves as a messenger carrying information encoded by the cell's **DNA** to help synthesize proteins, enzymes, and hormones. In some **viruses**, including HIV and other **retroviruses**, **RNA** comprises the genes that contain the information necessary for invading **host** cells and viral replication.

Salmonella   A family of **bacteria** that cause disease and are spread through contaminated food, water, or food preparation surfaces.

USAMRID   United States Army Medical Research of Infectious Diseases; located at Fort Detrick, Frederick, Maryland.

vector   An organism, such as an insect or rodent, that transmits a **pathogen.**

virus   A parasitic organism that consists of a protein coat that encloses **DNA** or **RNA**. **Viruses** need living cells of **hosts** to replicate.

World Health Organization (WHO)   An agency of the United Nations charged with setting and promoting health standards and research.

For Further Discussion

Chapter 1

1. Malcolm Gladwell argues that the American people are "in the grip of paranoia about viruses and diseases" and feel "a sense of helplessness" about them. He cites Laurie Garrett's book as an example of such thinking. After reading the viewpoints of Garrett and Gladwell, do you believe that Garrett's arguments are realistic or, as Gladwell believes, overly pessimistic about the threat of diseases? Explain your answer.

2. Malcolm Gladwell contends that the 1983 epidemic in Pennsylvania that killed 17 million chickens should not be viewed as a possible indicator for a similar event affecting humans. What reasons does he give for rejecting the analogy between that event and the public health of the people? Do these reasons, in your judgment, provide sufficient grounds for agreeing with his conclusion? Why or why not?

3. Ed Regis argues that fears of a worldwide viral epidemic are overstated and result from a "revenge of the rain forest" conception that is not supported by the scientific evidence. Is this an accurate or misleading description of Frank Ryan's arguments about viruses? Explain your answer.

Chapter 2

1. Tom Coburn maintains that past AIDS public health policies have failed and must be changed. Mark S. Senak argues that past public health policies regarding AIDS might have to be changed given the success of new drug therapies, but he goes on to criticize proposals of Tom Coburn and others. After reading the two viewpoints, what do you believe are the fundamental sources of disagreement between the two about how to control the AIDS epidemic? Do you think there are elements of a new AIDS policy that both Senak and Coburn could agree upon? Explain.

2. Robert E. Stein argues that in response to AIDS, the ultimate bottom line, should be saving lives. However, W. Bradford Wilcox argues that needle exchange programs (NEPs) are unacceptable "even if NEPs do save thousands of lives in the short term." Is this statement evidence of fundamental philosophical differences between the authors? Explain.

3. What differences of opinion do Charles Krauthammer and H.R. Shepherd express about the spread of AIDS? Do you believe these disagreements stem from the fact that Shepherd focuses to a greater extent on AIDS cases outside the United States? Why or why not?

1. The Children's Defense Fund (CDF) focuses on the immunization rates of children and how they can be increased, while Russell Redenbaugh focuses on future needs for vaccine development. Can a vaccination policy be developed that addresses both concerns? Explain.

2. Both the Centers for Disease Control and Prevention (CDC) and Alan Philips set up their arguments by describing certain "myths" about vaccines that they seek to dispel. Do you find this an effective method of presenting their arguments? Which viewpoint did you find more convincing? Why?

3. The CDC is an integral part of America's medical establishment. Alan Philips has no formal medical training. How important is such background information in evaluating their viewpoints, in your judgment? Explain.

4. Both Alan Philips and Barbara Loe Fisher became interested in vaccinations following experiences with their own children. How relevant are these experiences to their arguments? Does the fact that they have a personal stake in the issue lend credence to their arguments or provide grounds for questioning their objectivity, in your view? Explain.

5. What arguments, characterizations, and descriptions does Arthur Allen make to discredit the anti-vaccination movement? Which do you find most convincing? Which to you find least convincing? After reading Fisher's viewpoint, do you agree or disagree with Allen's portrayal of her and her ideas? Why?

CHAPTER 4

1. Both the American Council on Science and Health (ASCH) and Nicols Fox argue that consumers must take personal action to ensure that their food is safe. What are the basic differences in the their respective recommendations? Is there a fundamental conflict between the two perspectives presented? Explain your answer.

2. What does John R. Cady find so threatening about the prospect of a "food czar"? In your opinion, do his arguments consist of scare tactics or rational objections to increased government regulation? How do his views towards government differ from those of Caroline Smith DeWaal?

3. Both John R. Cady and the ACSH stress that food cannot be made 100 percent risk free. What implications do they draw from this claim, and how does it relate to their arguments about government regulation?

4. Which of the arguments for and against irradiation made by Richard Rhodes, Michael Colby, and Michael F. Jacobson, do you find most convincing? Which do you find least convincing? After reading their arguments, would you be more or less likely to purchase food that has been irradiated versus the same product without the irradiation label? Explain your answer.

ORGANIZATIONS TO CONTACT

The editors have compiled the following list of organizations concerned with the issues debated in this book. The descriptions are derived from materials provided by the organizations. All have publications or information available for interested readers. The list was compiled on the date of publication of the present volume; the information provided here may change. Be aware that many organizations take several weeks or longer to respond to inquiries, so allow as much time as possible.

AIDS Coalition to Unleash Power (ACT UP/New York)

332 Bleecker St., G5, New York, NY 10014
phone/fax: (212) 966-4873
e-mail: actupny@panix.com • website: http://www.actupny.org

ACT UP is a group of individuals committed to direct action to end the AIDS crisis. Through education and demonstrations, ACT UP works to end discrimination; achieve adequate funding for AIDS research, health care, and housing for people with AIDS; and disseminate information about safer sex, clean needles, and other AIDS prevention methods. ACT UP publishes action manuals, such as *Time to Become an AIDS Activist*, and on-line action reports.

Alliance for the Prudent Use of Antibiotics (APUA)

PO Box 1372, Boston, MA 02117
(617) 636-0966 • fax: (617) 636-0458
e-mail: apua@apua.tufts.edu • website: http://www.healthsci.tufts.edu/apua

The alliance is a grassroots organization dedicated to research and education about appropriate antibiotic use. By advocating the prudent use of antibiotics, the APUA seeks to preserve the power of antibiotics by preventing the increase of pathogens' resistance to them. APUA publishes information pamphlets, a newsletter, and the video *Confronting Antibiotic Resistance: An Increasing Threat to Public Health*.

American Council on Science and Health (ACSH)

1995 Broadway, 2nd Fl., New York, NY, 10023-5860
(212) 362-7044 • fax: (212) 362-4919
website: http://www.acsh.org

ACSH is a consumer education consortium concerned with, among other topics, issues related to health and disease. ACSH publishes *Priorities* magazine and position papers such as *Facts Versus Fears: A Review of the Greatest Unfounded Health Scares of Recent Times*.

Center for Science in the Public Interest (CSPI)

1875 Connecticut Ave. NW, Suite 300, Washington, DC 20009
(202) 332-9110 • fax: (202) 265-4954
e-mail cspi@cspinet.org • website: http://www.cspinet.org

The center is a nonprofit education and advocacy organization that focuses on improving the safety and nutritional quality of America's food supply. The CSPI educates the public about nutrition and lobbies for food safety regulation in an attempt to ensure that advances in science are used for the public's good. It publishes the *Nutrition Action Healthletter* and organizes grassroots campaigns for food labeling and safety.

Centers for Disease Control and Prevention (CDC)

1600 Clifton Rd. NE, Atlanta, GA 30333
(404) 639-3311
e-mail: netinfo@cdc.gov • website: http://www.cdc.gov

The CDC is the government agency charged with protecting the public health of the nation by preventing and controlling diseases and by responding to public health emergencies. Programs of the CDC include the National Center for Infectious Diseases, which publishes *Addressing Emerging Infectious Disease Threats: A Prevention Strategy for the United States* and the journal *Emerging Infectious Diseases*, and the National Center for HIV, STD, and TB Prevention, which publishes the *HIV/AIDS Prevention Newsletter*. The CDC website also offers general news and educational information on many diseases and other health issues.

Federation of American Scientists

Program for Monitoring Emerging Diseases (ProMED)
307 Massachusetts Ave. NE, Washington, DC 20002
(202) 546-3300 • fax: (202) 675-1010
e-mail: fas@fas.org • website: http://www.fas.org/promed

The Federation of American Scientists is a privately funded, nonprofit organization engaged in analysis and advocacy on science, technology, and public policy for global security. ProMED seeks to link scientists, public health officials, journalists, and laypersons in a global communications network for reporting disease outbreaks. The federation requests that students and other researchers first investigate the resources available on its website, such as the papers *Controlling Infectious Diseases* and *Global Monitoring of Emerging Diseases: Design for a Demonstration Program*, before requesting further information.

Food and Drug Administration (FDA)
Center for Food Safety and Applied Nutrition

200 C St. SW, Washington, DC 20204
consumer information hot line: (800) 532-4440 or (301) 827-4420
websites: http://www.fda.gov • http://www.cfsan.fda.gov

Part of the U.S. Department of Health and Human Services, the FDA is a public health agency charged with protecting American consumers by, among other things, ensuring the safety and quality of food. The administration tests food samples for harmful substances, sets labeling standards to help consumers know what is in the foods they buy, and monitors the safety of feeds and other drugs given to food animals.

The FDA publishes many fact sheets and updates on food safety as well as the *Bad Bug Book* of food-borne pathogenic microorganisms.

Global Vaccine Awareness League

(415) 507-1504

e-mail: DQSA45A@prodigy.com • website: http://pages.prodigy.com/gval

The league is a nonprofit organization committed to educating parents and concerned citizens about the potential risks and serious side effects of vaccines. It publishes a newsletter, fact sheets about vaccines, books, videotapes, and pamphlets such as *Vaccines: Are They Really Safe and Effective?* and *Your Personal Guide to Immunization Exemptions.*

HIV/AIDS Treatment Information Service (ATIS)

PO Box 6303, Rockville, MD 20849-6303

(800) HIV-0440 (800-448-0440) • fax: (301) 519-6616

e-mail: atis@hivatis.org • website: http://www.hivatis.org

The HIV/AIDS Treatment Information Service provides information about federally approved treatment guidelines for HIV and AIDS. It publishes *Principles of Therapy of HIV Infection* as well as reports and guidelines for treating HIV infection in adults, adolescents, and children.

National AIDS Fund

1400 I St. NW, Suite 1220, Washington, DC 20005

(202) 408-4848 • fax: (202) 408-1818

e-mail: info@aidsfund.org • website: http://www.aidsfund.org

The National AIDS Fund seeks to eliminate HIV as a major health and social problem. Its members work in partnership with the public and private sectors to provide care and to prevent new infections in communities and in the workplace by means of advocacy, grants, research, and education. The fund publishes the monthly newsletter *News from the National AIDS Fund.*

National Coalition for Adult Immunization (NCAI)

4733 Bethesda Ave., Suite 750, Bethesda, Maryland 20814

(301) 656-0003 • fax: (301) 907-0878

e-mail: adultimm@aol.org • website: http://www.medscape.com/affiliates/ncai

NCAI is a nonprofit organization composed of more than ninety-five professional medical and health care associations, advocacy groups, voluntary organizations, vaccine manufacturers, and government health agencies. The common goal of all members is to improve the immunization status of adults and adolescents to levels specified by the U.S. Public Health Service. Annually, NCAI publishes the *Resource Guide for Adult and Adolescent Immunization* and spearheads the *National Adult Immunization Awareness Week* (NAIAW) campaign in October.

National Foundation for Infectious Diseases

4733 Bethesda Ave., Suite 750, Bethesda, Maryland 20814
(301) 656-0003 • fax: (301) 907-0878
e-mail: nfid@aol.com • website: http://www.nfid.org

The foundation is a nonprofit philanthropic organization that supports disease research through grants and fellowships and educates the public about research, treatment, and prevention of infectious diseases, including AIDS. It publishes a newsletter, *Double Helix*, and its website contains a "Virtual Library of Diseases."

National Institute of Allergy and Infectious Diseases (NIAID)

NIAID Office of Communications, Building 31, Room 7A-50
31 Center Dr. MSC 2520, Bethesda, MD 20892-2520
website: http://www.niaid.nih.gov

The institute, one of the programs of the National Institutes of Health, supports scientists conducting research on infectious, immunologic, and allergic diseases that afflict people worldwide. Emerging diseases and AIDS constitute two of NIAID's main areas of research, and many materials are available from NIAID on these topics, including *Emerging Infectious Diseases Research: Meeting the Challenge* and *The Relationship Between HIV and AIDS*.

National Vaccine Information Center

512 W. Maple Ave., Suite 206, Vienna, VA 22180
(800) 909-SHOT • (703) 938-0342 • fax: (703) 938-5768
e-mail: info@909shot.com • website: http://www.909shot.com

The center is dedicated to the prevention of vaccine injuries and deaths through public education. It is operated by Dissatisfied Parents Together, a national nonprofit educational organization that advocates reforming the mass vaccination system. The center distributes information on vaccine safety and on reporting adverse effects after vaccination, and it publishes the book *The Consumer's Guide to Childhood Vaccines*.

Safe Tables Our Priority (STOP)

335 Court St., Suite 100, Brooklyn, NY 11231
(718) 246-2739 • fax: (718) 624-4267
e-mail: feedback@stop-usa.org • website: http://www.stop-usa.org

STOP is a nonprofit grassroots organization that seeks to prevent unnecessary illness and loss of life from pathogenic food-borne illness. It offers victim assistance, educates the public, and advocates regulatory reforms in order to ensure safe food and public health. STOP distributes information for victims of food-borne illness and issues press releases on food safety developments.

U.S. Department of Agriculture (USDA)

14th and Independence Ave. SW, Washington, DC 20250
(202) 720-2791
websites: http://www.usda.gov • http://www.fsis.usda.gov
National Food Safety Database: http://www.foodsafety.org

The USDA is responsible for supporting U.S. agricultural production. The Food Safety and Inspection Service, a USDA agency, is responsible for ensuring that the nation's commercial supply of meat, poultry, and egg products is safe, wholesome, and correctly labeled and packaged. The USDA publishes many guidelines and fact sheets on food safety, and it is the primary funder of the National Food Safety Database.

BIBLIOGRAPHY OF BOOKS

Karen Bellenir and Peter D. Dresser, eds. *Food and Animal Borne Diseases Sourcebook.* Detroit: Omnigraphics, 1995.

Wayne Biddle *A Field Guide to Germs.* New York: Henry Holt, 1995.

Elinor Burkett *The Gravest Show on Earth: America in the Age of AIDS.* Boston: Houghton Mifflin, 1995.

William E. Burrows and Robert Windrem *Critical Mass: The Dangerous Race for Superweapons in a Fragmenting World.* New York: Simon & Schuster, 1994.

William R. Clark *At War Within: The Double-Edged Sword of Immunity.* New York: Oxford University Press, 1995.

Leonard A. Cole *The Eleventh Plague: The Politics of Biological and Chemical Warfare.* New York: W.H. Freeman, 1997.

Peter H. Duesberg *Inventing the AIDS Virus.* Washington, DC: Regnery, 1996.

Gail A. Eisnitz *Slaughterhouse: The Shocking Story of Greed, Neglect, and Inhumane Treatment Inside the U.S. Meat Industry.* Amherst, NY: Prometheus Books, 1997.

Nicols Fox *Spoiled: The Dangerous Truth About a Food Chain Gone Haywire.* New York: BasicBooks, 1997.

Laurie Garrett *The Coming Plague: Newly Emerging Diseases in a World out of Balance.* New York: Farrar, Strauss, & Giroux, 1994.

Nancy Goldstein and Jennifer L. Manlowe, eds. *The Gender Politics of HIV/AIDS in Women: Perspectives on the Pandemic in the United States.* New York: New York University Press, 1997.

Robin Gorna *Vamps, Virgins, and Victims: How Can Women Fight AIDS?* London: Cassell, 1996.

Lawrence O. Gostin and Zita Lazzarini *Human Rights and Public Health in the AIDS Pandemic.* New York: Oxford University Press, 1997.

Henry Grabowski and John Vernon *The Search for New Vaccines: The Effects of the Vaccines for Children Program.* Washington, DC: AEI Press, 1997.

Christine Grady *The Search for an AIDS Vaccine: Ethical Issues in the Development and Testing of a Preventive HIV Vaccine.* Bloomington: Indiana University Press, 1995.

Robin Marantz Henig *A Dancing Matrix: How Science Confronts Emerging Viruses.* New York: Vintage Books, 1994.

Leonard G. Horowitz *Emerging Viruses: AIDS and Ebola: Nature, Accident, or Intentional?* Rockport, MA: Tetrahedron, 1996.

Walene James *Immunization: The Reality Behind the Myth.* South Hadley, MA: Bergin & Garvey, 1995.

Arno Karlen *Man and Microbes: Disease and Plagues in History and Modern Times.* New York: G.P. Putnam's Sons, 1995.

Jeffrey A. Kelly *Changing HIV Risk Behavior: Practical Strategies.* New York: Guilford, 1995.

George C. Kohn, ed.	Encyclopedia of Plague and Pestilence. New York: Facts On File, 1995.
Richard M. Krause, ed.	Emerging Infections (Biomedical Research Reports). San Diego: Academic, 1998.
Marc Lappe	Evolutionary Medicine: Rethinking the Origins of Disease. San Francisco: Sierra Club Books, 1994.
Joshua Lederberg, Robert E. Shope, and Stanley C. Oaks, eds.	Emerging Infections: Microbial Threats to Human Health in the United States. Washington, DC: National Academy Press, 1992.
Myron Levine et al.	New Generation Vaccines. New York: Marcel Dekker, 1997.
Joseph B. McCormick and Susan Fisher-Hoch	Level 4: Virus Hunters of the CDC. Atlanta: Turner, 1996.
Randall Neustaedter	The Vaccine Guide: Making an Informed Choice. Berkeley, CA: North Atlantic Books, 1996.
Jacques Normand, David Vlahov, and Lincoln E. Moses, eds.	Preventing HIV Transmission: The Role of Sterile Needles and Bleach. Washington, DC: National Academy Press, 1995.
C.J. Peters and Mark Olshaker	Virus Hunter: Thirty Years of Battling Hot Viruses Around the World. New York: Anchor, 1997.
Josh Powell	AIDS and HIV-Related Diseases: An Educational Guide for Professionals and the Public. New York: Insight Books, 1996.
Richard Preston	The Hot Zone. New York: Random House, 1994.
Sheldon Rampton and John Stauber	Mad Cow U.S.A.: Could the Nightmare Happen Here? Monroe, ME: Common Courage Press, 1997.
Ed Regis	Virus Ground Zero: Stalking the Killer Viruses with the Centers for Disease Control. New York: Pocket Books, 1996.
Richard Rhodes	Deadly Feasts: Tracking the Secrets of a Terrifying New Plague. New York: Simon & Schuster, 1997.
Eric Rofes	Reviving the Tribe: Regenerating Gay Men's Sexuality and Culture in the Ongoing Epidemic. New York: Haworth Press, 1996.
Bernard Roizman	Infectious Diseases in an Age of Change: The Impact of Human Ecology and Behavior on Disease Transmission. Washington, DC: National Academy Press, 1995.
Gabriel Rotello	Sexual Ecology: AIDS and the Destiny of Gay Men. New York: E.P. Dutton, 1997.
Mark S. Senak	A Fragile Circle. Los Angeles: Alyson, 1998.
Mark S. Senak	HIV, AIDS, and the Law: A Guide to Our Rights and Challenges. New York: Insight Books, 1996.
Paul D. Stolley and Tamar Lasky	Investigating Disease Patterns: The Science of Epidemiology. New York: Scientific American Library, 1995.
Christopher Wills	Yellow Fever, Black Goddess: The Coevolution of People and Plagues. Reading, MA: Helix Books, 1996.

INDEX